5/24

PRAISE FOR BL~~EST~~ ~~~~

As a historian, Deborah Sweaney placed her first two books into historical context, causing the reader to understand how local events and people connect to larger, national history. *Blest Be the Tie* is no exception. It is both an intimate portrayal of four generations of women whose lives, experiences and strength helped shape America, and a history of a particular time and place. Sweaney makes one appreciate the extraordinary lives of 'ordinary' people.

> – Cathy Gorn, Ph.D.
> Executive Director, National History Day

Deborah has written the story that so many of us have dreamed of writing; the story of our mothers and grandmothers. The story we want so desperately to pass down to our daughters and granddaughters so they will know – truly know – the women who came before. She has told the story of her mothers. It is also the story of a multitude of women from the "greatest" generations. Our daughters should read it. Our granddaughters should heed it.

> – Laura Bullion
> Former Archivist, State Historical Society of Missouri

I absolutely love *Blest Be the Tie*. Deborah Sweaney has done a remarkable job. I especially like the way she interweaves the stories of her family with the larger historical context, and connects that context to her own life. Blest Be the Tie illustrates how history is personal for all of us as the effects of events are passed down to us as part of our family legacy. I think all serious students of history should read the book to better understand this personal connection we all have with the past. Historians often talk about how the event of the past continue to shape the present, but they rarely seem to address the role of family as a major conduit for the influence of history on individuals. Well done!

- Jeffrey Hawks
Education Director, Army Heritage Center Foundation

Blest Be the Tie is a fascinating story of four generations of the author's family, especially its women. Reading it is like opening an old cedar chest and finding letters and pictures saved by people who could well have been one's own family members. Future academic historians will use anecdotes and quotes from this book to illustrate their generalizations, but anyone who just likes good stories will enjoy it now. Deborah Sweaney has done a remarkable job of meeting the challenges of highly personal story-telling. She isn't afraid to mention her own feelings, but never slips into mere sentimentalizing. She provides historical context with a deft touch and eye for detail. She notes the social and economic limits within which her mother, grandmother and great-grandmother lived but avoids editorializing. We come to share her admiration for these women's courage, as well as her own evident pleasure at their successes.

- Fred D. Baldwin
Ph.D., American History

Blest Be the Tie is a captivating account through four generations of courageous women and their families. Reading it feels like entering another world -- where the characters and history come to life. The book has extra charm for Laura Ingalls Wilder fans, as it closely parallels Laura's life, and brings back memories of reading the Little house series.

- Amy Garcia
First Grade teacher and a Laura Fan

Anna, Carrie, Iris; in fact all the members of Deborah's family became very real to me through the pages of *Blest Be the Tie*. Their stories resonated with me, and through them I gained a greater appreciation of the legacy passed on to me by the women in my own family.

– Robin Atwood Fidler
Former museum educator, Maryland Historical Society

Through effortless storytelling, Sweaney allows the reader to feel like they are a part of key events in American history, from the Panic of 1893 and the Great Depression to World War II and the Baby Boom. One will feel like they can identify with the women of Sweaney's past as the events of time unfold. And the reader will come to realize, as Sweaney aptly notes, that "our actions can ripple across generations." After reading *Blest Be the Tie*, one will find themselves wanting to know more about their own family's past and realize how familial ties create a strong link to the past while creating a sturdy bridge to the future. For Sweaney tells us that "Life does not always follow a direct path…there are curves on the road and bumps along the way….there are detours that take us away from our intended destination." It is these curves, bumps, and detours that make Sweaney's ancestors' story the American story. Her craft at storytelling make *Blest Be the Tie* an enjoyable and thought-provoking work, no matter what age the reader may be.

– Kevin Wagner
Recipient of the 2017 Christa McAuliffe Reach for the Stars Award, National Council for the Social Studies

Blest Be the Tie

The Story of an American Family

Deborah Sweaney

WORD ASSOCIATION PUBLISHERS
www.wordassociation.com
1.800.827.7903

The Author's Missouri Trilogy:

Unpacking Memories

Up In The Air

Blest Be The Tie

Copyright © 2017 by Deborah Sweaney

All rights reserved. No part of this book/manuscript may be reproduced in any form or by any electronic or mechanical means, including information or storage and retrieval systems, without permission in writing from the author.

Printed in the United States of America.

ISBN: 978-1-63385-231-0

Library of Congress Control Number: 2017917324

Designed and published by

Word Association Publishers
205 Fifth Avenue
Tarentum, Pennsylvania 15084

www.wordassociation.com
1.800.827.7903

For Kelly, who loved my mother,
and
for Ruth, who did not have a chance to read this book.

The illustrations in this book were drawn by Carrie Elsie Swartz before her marriage to Finn McCluey on February 21, 1911.

Writing depends on who your grandmother is.
Maxim Gorky, Russian writer

Table of Contents

Appreciation

I have been blessed with three siblings: Lou Ann, Jim, and Carry. We are tied together by love and shared memories. You can read about their births in the following pages. I also have an extended family of cousins who were central to creating this book. Great-grandchildren of Robert and Sarah McCluey and George and Anna Swartz contributed not only their stories, but, in some cases, they lent me family treasures. I hope you will take the time to read the notes in the back of this book to learn about their contributions.

Writing this book was not only daunting, but at times a painful and emotional journey. There were two people who never saw McCluey land who encouraged me. Without them, I might not have had the courage to finish the story. First, my dear friend, Dr. Cathy Gorn, the Executive Director of National History Day, believed in this book. She was there with laughter, encouragement, and more than one glass of champagne. She brought out her red pen to correct my sentence structure. Just as we remind History Day Students, she told me more than once to always remember that "historic context and analysis" are always worth the most points.

Jim Baker, my husband, lived with me during the creation of this book. It was not always easy to do. He was my supporter, encourager, editor, and toward the end of the process, my typist. He helped rework some of my sentences and even drafted more than one. I treasure him more than words can say.

Preface

This is a work of nonfiction. Anna, Carrie, and Iris lived America's story. Each one was of her time, affected by the events of her day that we now call history. Their lives were nothing special. There were women like them in most American families. They just happen to be in my family.

This book is not a collection of family lore. The stories of these women and their husbands did not occur in a vacuum. Historic events, popular culture, and scientific advances are interwoven with the personal stories to add context and depth. I studied works of noted historians for facts and insights into issues dominating their lives. I read scholarly essays on Coxey's Army and other books about the depression that rocked America during the 1890s. Newspapers from Des Moines, Iowa, and Lockwood, Missouri, provided glimpses into another time and place. Statistics from the University of Missouri in 1946 were not just dry numbers, but provided historic context to my parent's newlywed years. I became a little angry reading propaganda from the Kansas City, Fort Scott and Memphis Railroad written in 1894. The railroad's description of the bountiful land of the Missouri Ozarks did not match the rocky soil.

I read diaries and memoirs written by women who lived at the same time as Anna and Carrie. Some of the women's names were unknown to me, but one was not: Laura Ingalls Wilder. I saw my great-grandparents' world through her diary, published as *On the Way Home*. She kept it during her 1894 trip from South Dakota to the Missouri Ozarks, with husband, Almanzo, and seven-year-old daughter Rose. Anna and her husband, George Washington Swartz, and their daughter, Carrie, were on the road to Missouri at the same time as Laura. Laura's words described the world both couples saw. With a copy of a deed and a modern GPS system, I was able to stand on the Iowa field where my great-grandfather planted corn in 1894. I picked up a handful of the rich black soil. It is now in a jar on my desk. It is a reminder that our actions can ripple across generations.

Laura's diary took me back to my own childhood and how much the *Little House on the Prairie* books meant to me as a girl. On one cold, wintry day in Pennsylvania, I relived the cold harshness of a Dakota winter. I opened my worn copy of *These Happy Golden Years* and quickly became lost in the romance of Laura Ingalls and her future husband Almanzo Wilder. My thoughts left the pages of the book and turned to the story of George Washington and Anna Swartz, my great-grandparents. The two families' experiences were so similar.

Pulitzer Prize winning historians brought Iris's teenage years into focus. I was inspired by the recorded voice of Franklin Delano Roosevelt delivering a fireside chat. Newspaper accounts provided temperature readings from the summer of 1934 and 1936. I recalled Steinbeck's fictional Joad family in *The Grapes of Wrath*. However, Anna and those like her who traveled Route 66 to California were not fictional creations.

Seldom do we have a chance to see our parents as young adults and to live their courtship days. I was able to do so last summer. I read the love letters my parents wrote to each other during World War II. They are full of the thoughts and activities of an ordinary G.I. and his girl who was living on the home front. Historians provided details on the Aleutian Islands Campaign and on the strategic importance of the Panama Canal. I listened to the romantic ballads that my father heard on Armed Services Radio. But it was Frank Sweaney's words and his insights that captured the time. I never really had a chance to know my father. I understand now why he was the love of my mother's life. Like her, I fell in love with him through his letters.

When I put my father's last letter, written in November 1945, back in its airmail envelope, I sat quietly. He was coming home full of love, dreams, and excitement. He was full of optimism and hope not only for his future with Iris, but also for the world. I knew the joys and sorrows of his life. Frank and Iris had only fifteen years together. I thought not only of my parents' story, but of the world events that had taken place over the last seventy years. History sometimes can be painful.

Deborah Sweaney
  Carlisle, PA
  January 2017

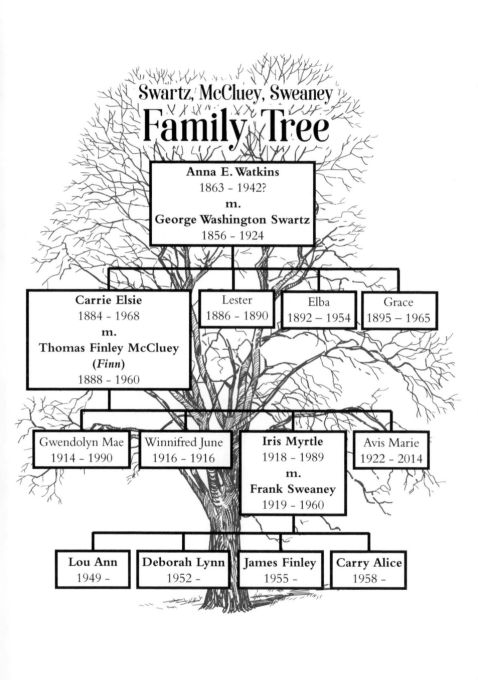

Swartz, McCluey, Sweaney
Family Tree

Anna E. Watkins
1863 – 1942?
m.
George Washington Swartz
1856 – 1924

Carrie Elsie
1884 – 1968
m.
Thomas Finley McCluey
(*Finn*)
1888 – 1960

Lester
1886 – 1890

Elba
1892 – 1954

Grace
1895 – 1965

Gwendolyn Mae
1914 – 1990

Winnifred June
1916 – 1916

Iris Myrtle
1918 – 1989
m.
Frank Sweaney
1919 – 1960

Avis Marie
1922 – 2014

Lou Ann
1949 –

Deborah Lynn
1952 –

James Finley
1955 –

Carry Alice
1958 –

This Is My Story;
This Is My Song

One

I held the drawing of the flower in my hand. It was on cheap paper, a pencil sketch drawn by a young girl in the last decade of the nineteenth century. I could almost touch the delicate iris blossom.

I have a framed picture of the girl who drew this flower. She is very pretty. I love the sound of her name: Carrie Elsie. It is soft and a little old-fashioned, like her drawing. It is clear that Carrie valued beauty. Her artwork is full of flowers and fashionable women. She must have loved these blossoms and wanted them in her life, for Carrie chose to name my mother, her middle daughter, after this flower.

I carry few physical features from my mother's mother. Carrie was small boned and short. At barely five feet four inches, I tower above the women in my family. I inherited my bone structure from my father. When I look at pictures from his family, I see my eyes staring back at me. The gifts that I get from my maternal line are less obvious. It is the life experiences of the women in my mother's family that I carry with me.

My story did not start the day I was born in 1952. It started centuries ago in the Scottish lowlands. It grew out of thirsty cornfields cracking from the lack of water in 1894, and by dry dirt blowing in the scorching heat of Missouri during the Dust Bowl. I am influenced by the actions of people who were born a century earlier than me and affected by their children who died before they had a chance to become adults. The Great Depression ended a decade before I was born, but those hard times influenced my life. I was created by my parents, who fell in love while writing letters to each other during World War II. I did not live these stories, but they are part of my soul.

The women who came before me were not independent creatures who controlled all aspects of their existence. I cannot tell their stories without telling of their husbands and fathers. These men made monumental decisions that changed the lives of their wives and daughters. Their lives were altered by wars fought in countries they would never visit and by actions of greedy and powerful men who lived in faraway cities. They believed in a God who controlled the flow of the sea and the moisture in the clouds; a God who, in his infinite wisdom, decided who lived or who died. The women reacted to events but never gave in to them. They kept going through hard times, droughts, and depression.

The girl in the picture frame is not the grandmother that I remember. My grandmother was an old woman. The young Carrie was lost, changed by poverty and hard work. But she existed once. I know because I have her drawings. This is her story and the story of her mother, Anna, and her daughter, Iris.

I am drawn to these women: to Anna's resilience, to Carrie's creativity, and to Iris's perseverance. Since my story starts with their story, perhaps it is my story as well.

Two

I do not write because I loved Grandma Carrie. Perhaps I need to tell her story, because I did not really love her when I was a child.

I knew I was supposed to love my grandma. But, truthfully, she seemed more of a bother than a blessing to me. She was just another responsibility for my mother, Iris. She came to live in our house after her husband died. I was eight that year. She was hard of hearing, a disability that seemed to lock her inside her body and limit her interaction with the kids that were always running past her. She sat in her chair in our living room, combing her pretty long hair, twisting it into a bun, and pinning it in place with crooked bobby pins. It was her ritual, her attempt at putting her life in order each day.

Order was impossible that winter of 1961. Death always brings disorder. My father had died the previous summer, leaving behind four small children and his widow. In the twenty-first century, we talk about death and the grief that follows it in clinical terms. "The stages of grief" sound so intellectual when you read about them. To move on, you must pass through denial, depression, anger, and some other stages described in self-help books. Those other stages do not really matter when I think about my childhood. It is depression that I remember when I think about that time.

In the Victorian era, a black wreath was placed on a door to acknowledge death. People who lived in our town did not need a wreath to remind them that my father was gone. He had been their doctor. "How could God take Doc Sweaney away so young? He was barely forty!" they mourned. They still needed him. He had delivered their babies, set their broken bones, and listened to their complaints. They were drawn to him not just for his caregiving, but for his personality. There were always people around him, like flies to honey. When my father was alive, they came to our house at all hours wanting his care. Our house was quiet now. The phone had stopped ringing, and no one knocked on the door in the middle of the night with a medical emergency. Our life was changed irrevocably by the God that lived in the open Bible that Grandma Carrie always seemed to have on her lap.

By that winter, the town people may have forgotten that our family suffered a double loss during that horrible hot July. Two weeks after Iris McCluey Sweaney buried her husband, her father died. I may not have been close to my grandmother, but I loved Grandpa McCluey. He paid attention to me, teased me, made me laugh, and gave me vanilla wafers. The two most important men in my mother's and my life were gone. I do not remember crying, but I cannot forget the overwhelming sense of sadness that permeated our house. The year that Grandma Carrie came to live with us, laughter died along with my father and grandfather.

If our life seemed out of control, then what must Grandma have felt? She was a stranger in a strange land. It had been only a year earlier that my McCluey grandparents moved to our town. Their health was failing, and it was clear they should no longer live by themselves. Their home was in the middle of nowhere. It was cold in the winter, and they had no electricity or indoor plumbing. My parents were too far away to take care of them, and there were no neighbors to check to see if they needed help. Everyone came to terms with the situation. It made sense for them to live closer to us. So my grandparents moved two hundred and fifty miles from their home in the Ozark foothills, where they had spent their married life. My parents rented a small house for them so they could maintain a sense of independence. They had modern conveniences but no friends. Even as a child, I knew that it was not an easy transition for my grandparents. When Grandpa died the following year, my mother moved Grandma into our home.

Her presence in our house was part of the "new normal" evolving for our family. I liked the old normal much better. More than half a century later, I push back tears when I think about that time. I am no longer a child of eight. I write now as a woman twenty–three years older than my mother was then, much closer to Grandma's age than hers. I can now see Grandma as a woman who was also grieving the loss of her husband.

Grandma Carrie belonged to another time and seemed out of place in the new world that was emerging in America in the 1960s. My grandmother did not engage in casual conversation during the years that she lived with us; however, sometimes she made a matter-of-fact observation, so absolutely true, one could only wonder why everyone had not said it before her. I remember one such incident. The Vietnam War was fought in our living room each night. "Body count" numbers were graphically displayed on the television news, indicating how many enemy combatants had been killed that day. It seemed as if the government was just trying to convince us with these numbers that the war was winnable.

I can still hear Grandma Carrie say, "If we are killing so many people, how can there be any Vietnamese left to kill us?"

I thought, *You know, she's right.* Obviously, she was more aware of the world around her than I gave her credit.

However, any emotions that she felt during those years were buried someplace deep inside her. Unlike the extroverted figures that bore the Sweaney name, Grandma was an introvert.

Three

If my grandparents missed South Missouri, my mother was eager to leave it. She was still bruised by childhood memories. She had thought the poverty and the social stigma of her early years were forever behind her. With dad gone and four children to support, she again was forced to worry about money.

When I tell my friends that my father was a doctor, they automatically assume that I had a privileged childhood. By the late 1950s, doctors reached a level of status in American society that was perhaps only rivaled by lawyers. Money usually came along with this status. People who make this assumption did not know or understand my father. He was never motivated by money. His three dollar standard fee for an office visit was just not that important to him and was often casually waived. I have no idea how often he actually collected money from those nightly house calls. Sometimes, his generosity got the best of him. His choices were not always practical, but they made him beloved. They also meant that our family had very little financial stability.

My mother postponed her own education to help put my father through medical school. Her decisions were not completely unselfish. My parents shared the dream of my father becoming a doctor. In no way should somebody assume that my mother was subservient. She was the strongest person that I have ever known. Hers was a quiet strength based always on reality. She did not tilt at windmills. She took what life gave her, kept her eyes on the future, and worked hard. But in 1961, those earlier decisions controlled her current options.

My parents did not often fight, but there was one time that Mom stood her ground. It happened a few years before I was born. Dad was finishing up his work as an intern at a large hospital in Memphis. He wanted to return to Missouri. He was not drawn to the city and wanted to be a country doctor. It looked like everything was falling in place for him. Back in the Ozark Hills, one of the doctors was retiring. His practice was there for the taking. For my dad, it seemed to be a tailor-made, God-given, opportunity. His family wanted him to come home. His wife had a different vision for their life. She remembered the cold and hunger of her childhood. Iris did not want to return to the Ozarks. She started crying and did not stop for the three days it took for Frank to give in. So instead of going home, they moved to the town of Oregon, in Northwest Missouri, and left the land of their childhood behind. The rich farmland of Northwest Missouri fostered a different culture than that of the Ozark Mountains.

Miles do not always distance us from our childhood. Mom's memories of the hard years of the Great Depression were always there. With Dad gone, they seemed to overwhelm her. Grief and anxiety brought the past to the present, and her Scots-Irish heritage took over. The McClueys fled the Ulster Plantation in Northern Island in the 1830s and brought their stern Scots Covenanter traditions to America. Iris carried their blood in her veins. She was raised on land settled by McClueys before the Civil War, and three centuries of memories lived in the McCluey home. As the Old Testament scribe knew, the actions of the fathers are "visited on the children, and the children's children, unto the third and to the fourth generation."

Faith flowed from the Old Testament. The Sunday sermon was often over before the preacher remembered that Jesus talked of love, not judgment. God was in control of life. After all, there better be a God who had a plan for your life because if not, what was the point? Life was not easy. It was hard to make a living from the rocky soil of the Ozark foothills. But it was McCluey land. You never took anything from anyone else. You worked for what you had. You paid your bills, never took charity, and above all else, you kept your commitments. If you had to borrow from the bank because of the depression that rocked the country during the thirties, then you had to work twice as hard to pay off the loan. Debt was such a serious business that the Lord had mentioned it in his prayer that you said each day: "Forgive us our debts, as we forgive our debtors."

Unlike her husband, Carrie Elsie Swartz McCluey was not born on the land where she raised her children. Her father, George Washington Swartz, was born in America, but his father came to America from a land where German was spoken. It was not uncommon for the Pennsylvania Dutch to name their sons after our first president. The Swartz family was Protestant and followed German Reformed doctrines. No McCluey would have considered marrying a Catholic. There were still too many memories of violence against their ancestors carried out in the name of that religion; however, not all Protestants followed the strict traditions practiced by the conservative Presbyterians of Scotland.

The one thing I know for sure about Grandma Carrie's father is that in the 1890s, he made one of the worst business decisions possible. He traded his rich Iowa land, sight unseen, for land in Southwest Missouri. The move to Missouri set the stage for Carrie's life. It did not seem fair to me that my Great-Grandfather Swartz made such a decision for his wife and daughters. They would have been rich had they stayed in Iowa, since an acre of Iowa land sells for an astronomical price. Its deep, dark, black soil is meant to be tilled and turned into fields of tall corn. Land is not created equal, and Southwest Missouri's soil is different. No one writes songs about corn climbing to the sky in that rocky soil.

Instead of living in poverty in the Ozark foothills, I wished for Carrie the life that she depicted in her drawings. I rewrote her story in my mind. In my version, her father did not leave Iowa. Instead, he stayed and prospered. Their farm was even better than the farms in Northwest Missouri where my schoolmates lived. I pictured a Currier and Ives world. I always imagined the 1890s to be such a romantic time. Did not books refer to the period as the Gay Nineties?

In my imagination, Carrie Swartz wore her hair like the women in her pictures and laughed gaily. She, along with her sisters Elba and Grace, went on sleigh rides behind beautiful horses singing "Jingle Bells." Their hands were protected from the cold by warm fur muffs. Her pretty long velvet dresses with bustles, sashes, and leg-of-mutton sleeves were in colors of forest green and rose. There were no droughts and economic downturns in my make-believe story of Grandma Carrie's life. And fathers always made careful and wise decisions.

But then she would not have been my grandmother, because Grandma Carrie would not have met my grandfather.

Four

Grandma left our house every six months or so to live with her youngest daughter Avis. Those weeks with Aunt Avis seemed to be a more comfortable living arrangement for Grandma Carrie. There was so much sadness and disorder in our house. The six-month rotation continued for several years, but then the challenges of caring for an elderly parent became too much for her daughters. Home care was no longer viable. Mom and Aunt Avis decided to move Grandma to a nursing home close to Aunt Avis's house in St. Joseph, thirty miles away from our home.

Mom piled us into the car on Sunday afternoons to drive to St. Joe to visit Grandma. I hated those visits. There was nothing to do, and by then, Grandma did not leave her bed. The smells of the care facility were overwhelming, and for a young girl, they were a little frightening. Carrie Elsie Swartz McCluey waited out her final days in that facility. She died in 1968 at the age of 84, having lived eight years as a widow.

She was buried beside her husband in the cemetery in Oregon. It never seemed to be the appropriate resting place for my grandparents. But I understood how it had happened that they were buried so far from McCluey land. My parents rest on the other side of my McCluey grandparents. The dates on the gravestones, so close together, chronicling Grandpa and Dad's deaths, tell the story. My mother bought family burial plots earlier that month. Grandpa was laid beside the other important man in her life.

There is nothing on Grandma Carrie's gravestone that tells anything about her. Only her name and the dates of her birth and death are etched on the marble. No one could know that the woman buried there was once a young girl who drew pictures of flowers and pretty women.

Five

The years moved on and my busy professional life left little time to dwell on family stories. In a doctor's office in suburban Washington, D.C., in April of 2003, Grandma Carrie's image came back to me.

I drove by the Tidal Basin on my way to the doctor's office that morning. The cherry trees were in full bloom, and pretty colorful tulips decorated the statutes honoring Civil War generals. Our nation's capital does Spring well. When I was growing up, I never understood the poet's fascination with that season. March and April are seldom pretty months in Northwest Missouri. The damp cold has a way of hanging on, and winter does not want to leave just because the calendar says that it is over.

As I crossed the Potomac into Northern Virginia, I momentarily looked to the south. I saw the Pentagon and briefly remembered the smoke that I had seen rising from it on September 11, 2001. Clearly, the twenty-first century was going to be very different than my childhood days in rural Missouri. I quickly pushed the image of the day of terror out of my mind. I had a more pressing and personal issue to worry about on that spring day. I had to face a growing health problem. I was losing my hearing.

I lived in a bureaucratic world where professional status was conveyed by invitations to meetings. Too often, the agenda did not "amount to a hill of beans," but the invitation conveyed prestige. I mastered the art of lip reading and positioned myself across from the power players. Thus, I was able to follow the conversation and hide my growing disability. However, two weeks earlier, an incident scared me. I realized I could no longer ignore the problem.

There was still a chill in the air that previous morning when I drove to work. I closed my car windows and was lost in thought as I planned my day in my head. I stopped behind another car and the light ahead changed to green. I impatiently honked my car horn to alert the driver of the light change. Then I saw the emergency vehicle, lights flashing, speed through the intersection. I had not heard the siren. The reality was that I or someone else could be dead if I had been driving the car ahead of me. Still shaking when I got to my office, I immediately searched the internet for a medical specialist and picked up the phone to make an appointment.

Now I was sitting in front of the well regarded doctor. I was nervous. I had spent the previous hour in a sound-proof booth, pressing a button as if I were on the game show Jeopardy; however, instead of jumping in with the correct answer, which I did with great success in my living room each night, I failed to press the button appropriately when the audiologist piped sounds into the booth. The doctor showed me the graph that mapped my hearing test. He explained my type of hearing loss. It is caused by calcium deposits around the small stapes bone in the middle ear. These deposits keep the bone from vibrating, thus inhibiting the transmission of the sound waves. There was good news though. With surgery, doctors can replace the stiff inflexible bone with a piece of Teflon, thereby correcting the deficiency.

I felt such relief. I could handle the idea of surgery. We compared our busy calendars and scheduled the procedure. Our conversation became more relaxed.

The doctor asked, "Is there hearing loss in your family?"

I pictured Grandma Carrie sitting in her chair, combing her long hair.

"Well, yes, my grandmother was hard of hearing," I said.

"Which grandmother?" the doctor asked.

"My mother's mother," I said.

"I expected that would be the case," he said. "For some reason that we do not understand, this type of hearing loss is almost always genetic, and it seems to be passed down in the maternal line."

Six

I graduated from college in 1974 and moved to Washington, D.C., to work as an intern for my congressman. Although I did not intend to do so, I stayed for the next thirty years, leaving my rural childhood behind. During my college years, the world changed. Smart women were now defined by their careers, not their husbands. When I married in 1986, I very proudly retained my maiden name.

We left Washington, D.C, for a new life in 2006. The need for security in our nation's capital was becoming stifling, and the city ceased to be fun for me. We settled in Carlisle, a historic college community in the Cumberland Valley of Pennsylvania. My D.C. friends all thought I was moving to a small town. It did not feel that way to me. I knew how small a town could be. Carlisle, population 20,000, was a city when compared to Oregon, Missouri, which barely had 800 people. We bought a new home outside of town on land that was a cornfield a decade earlier.

My urban world faded into the background and I heard the call of rural America. I began to revisit my childhood in my mind. I was called to write and, daily, found myself reliving rural Missouri in the 1950s. I studied family papers and photos in my research for the book that became *Unpacking Memories*. It was a book primarily about my father; however, his pictures were not the only ones that caught my eye. There were black and white photos of my mother and Grandma Carrie from those years when they were both recent widows. I felt the sharp pain of that time, a pain that still existed below the surface, some place just below my heart.

Grandma Carrie's death certificate was folded among the family papers. I read the facts of her life. Her birth date of 1884 in Central Iowa jumped out at me. I knew Central Iowa. It was the heart of the Midwest, corn and soybeans. The long corn rows in the Cumberland Valley of Pennsylvania are short by comparison to Iowa fields. In Pennsylvania, we still have picturesque farms with animals. In Iowa, it is not so much about farms as farmland. For there, the land is so fertile that you see few buildings on it, only crops. My picture is of current day Iowa. Big, powerful machines plow the rich land instead of horses. My grandmother was born when automobiles and planes were science fiction—a world where Europe was ruled by Kaisers and Tsars.

I stumbled across some of Grandma Carrie's childhood drawings among the family papers. I looked at them in amazement. She was very talented. I saw her world in these drawings: horses pulling plows, and Gibson Girls with their hair arranged in pompadours. There obviously was no money for art paper because Carrie used any piece of paper that she could find for her sketches. There were drawings on envelopes and scrap paper. She decorated the borders of the pages from Big Chief tablets with fancy artwork. As to be expected, some of the drawings were a little primitive. I knew she had had no formal training. What would her life have been like in a different time and place? If she had lived in a time of medical advancement, when her hearing could have been corrected? In a world where creativity was not a luxury?

I remembered the story of her father trading his land. I thought, *What really happened those years so long ago?* Somehow, that decision set the course for his life and the life of his children and grandchildren. More than one hundred twenty years later, his great-grandchildren still shake their heads in wonder: *How could anyone have done that?*

My mother and grandmother's stories did not begin in my childhood house. Their lives started long before they grieved the death of their husbands. Could I piece together those events that set the stage for the life of these two women and, therefore, my own life? Was it possible to find out what really happened to the women who lived before me? It all starts with Great-Grandpa's decision to move his young family to Missouri.

I Am Bound for the Promised Land

Seven

George Washington Swartz heard the call, "Go West, young man." He was in his mid-twenties, living in Pennsylvania. There was new land for the taking out west. The year was 1879. The Civil War had been over for more than a decade and Americans were exuberant and optimistic. His young wife, Anna, joined him in this new adventure. George and Anna were part of America's destiny. After all, everyone just knew that our country was meant to reach all the way from the Atlantic to the Pacific. The government in Washington encouraged westward migration, with the promise of land ownership to people who homesteaded. The land would be theirs if they could manage to stick it out for five years.

I do not know much about Anna's family. There are no family stories passed down about them. Anna and George moved across the mountains of Pennsylvania, crossed the Ohio River, and joined the other westward pioneers in their covered wagons, rolling over the planted fields of Ohio and Illinois. On the other side of the Mississippi River, they found their land close to a small community east of Des Moines called Peoria. George attached his plow to his horse and planted corn. Their neighbors were German Reformed too. It must have felt like home to Anna and George. It was time to start a family. In 1884, their first child, Carrie, was born, followed two years later by a son, Lester. They had two more daughters, Elba and Grace, while living on those Iowa fields.

One hundred and thirty years later, I stood on this land. It was October, and the harvest was over. The big, powerful combine had already moved across the field, cutting the corn and separating the kernels from the ears. I picked up a handful of the black soil. I pictured the red rocky soil of Southwest Missouri. How could George leave this rich land? I wanted to understand this decision. The clues were there to unravel this mystery. Some were buried in scholarly American history books. I turned to them first. They helped me understand the times. But dusty tomes did not provide a window into George and Anna's life. I was surprised to find it in the writings of my favorite childhood author, Laura Ingalls Wilder.

Laura Ingalls Wilder wrote her classic *Little House* series of books as a woman in her sixties, looking back on her life as a pioneer girl. The stories are based on her experiences on the American frontier of the 1870s. She was born in 1867 in a log cabin in the *Little House in the Big Woods* of Wisconsin. Her parents, Charles and Caroline Ingalls, left Wisconsin with their daughters and illegally built a little house on the prairie, on land reserved for Indians in Kansas. The government removed them from the Kansas land and, subsequently, the Ingalls family moved around the Midwest. The books are told in third person, with Laura as the central character. She grows up in the pages of the eight books. Each covers a different time period of her life, and the title of several of the books call to mind the location of the stories. The last three books are set in De Smet, South Dakota, and feature the hero of the books, Almanzo Wilder. The original series ends with their marriage in the last pages of *These Happy Golden Years*.

A real life Laura and Almanzo existed outside of the childhood classics. It never occurred to me as a girl that they were contemporaries of my great-grandparents and that the two couples' early married experiences paralleled each other. Almanzo Wilder and George Swartz were born less than a year apart, George sometime in 1856 and Almanzo in February of 1857. They both left the East for land in the Upper Midwest in the 1870s. George settled in Central Iowa, and Almanzo eventually found his way to the neighboring state of South Dakota. Their daughters, Carrie Swartz and Rose Wilder, were born just a few years apart. In 1894, both men made the same monumental decision: Each moved his young family to South Missouri.

In spite of the cold and the hardships depicted in the books, Laura's stories appealed to my romantic nature. As a girl, I imagined that I was Laura. Almanzo became my first romantic hero. In my mind, he tucked the blanket around my legs to protect me from the freezing cold of a South Dakota winter. When Laura described her pearl engagement ring, I held out my left hand, picturing it on my ring finger. I saw myself as Laura, clinging to Almanzo against all the hardships: the heat, tornadoes, grasshoppers, and lack of rain. But we are always steadfast, watching the sun setting in the West each night, ready to face the new day when it rose again in the East. And after overcoming all the obstacles, we prospered from our land. That is my idyllic fantasy. It did not happen that way for Laura and Almanzo, and it did not happen that way for George and Anna.

I was not alone in my attachment to the *Little House* books. The books have legions of fans and spawned a popular television series. The sites where the Ingalls family lived have become tourist destinations, with gift shops that sell *Little*

House memorabilia. The *Little House* series is the subject of doctoral theses and scholarly books. Laura's life and her writings have been analyzed (perhaps a little overanalyzed) in academic journals. Everything she has ever written has been published. It is this material that offers insights into decisions made not only by Laura and Almanzo Wilder, but also by Charles and Anna Swartz.

Laura's original books ended with her marriage to Almanzo. She started another novel, *The First Four Years,* about their early married life. She wrote in hand on Big Chief tablet paper, just as she had drafted all her other classic children's stories. After Almanzo's death, she put this book away and did not finish it. It was found in 1968 in her daughter Rose's papers. When I look at this date, I am reminded that Rose was Grandma Carrie's contemporary. They both died in their eighties the same year.

I read this unedited novel shortly after it was published in 1971. Six years earlier, I left Laura and Almanzo in newlywed splendor in the little house that he had lovingly built for his new bride. My first reaction when I closed *The First Four Years* was that I wished that it had never been published. I wanted to live in the last lines of *These Happy Golden Years*:

"It is a wonderful night," Almanzo said.

"It is a beautiful world," Laura answered, and in her memory, she heard the voice of Pa's fiddle and the echo of a song,

> "Golden years are passing by,
> These happy, golden years."

Laura's world was not always beautiful. Neither was Anna Swartz's. Their harsh lives were governed by crop failures, little rain, and economic hardships. At times, their stories are incredibly sad. Each family buried a son during their early married years. The land that they dreamed would offer rich bounty was turned over to a grave. Neither father passed on his name through a son. Laura's infant son died in 1889. A year later, George and Anna buried their son, Lester, in the neighboring state of Iowa. They had him longer than Laura was able to keep her son. According to his gravestone, the son of G. W. and Anna Swartz died having lived four years, three months, and two days.

Anna and George picked out a pretty site five miles from their land for their young son. Other gravestones now surround little Lester's grave. I visited the well-maintained cemetery one hundred and twenty-five years after Anna and George placed the gravestone over the little boy's body. A gentle slope led down to a pasture where sheep were grazing. I pictured Anna holding six-year-old Carrie's hand as they placed flowers on her little brother's grave. Perhaps Carrie reached out to touch the etching on the stone that marked where Lester lay. But I cannot see tears on Anna's face. The women in my mother's family never showed their grief openly. Instead, they always kept private counsel. These women were like the biblical Madonna and pondered life events in their hearts.

When Laura writes of her reaction to the death of her infant son, I think of Anna Swartz, who left her second child in an Iowa grave:

> *Laura was doing her own work again one day three weeks later when the baby was taken with spasms, and he died so quickly that the doctor was too late. To Laura, the days that*

followed were mercifully blurred. Her feelings were numbed and she only wanted to rest—to rest and not to think.

George and Anna had little time at their son's gravesite. A farmer and his wife never have the luxury of retreating from work for very long. George returned to his fields, working his land behind horses. Anna cared for her daughters and everything else.

A farm is such a hard place for a woman. There are so many chores for her to do …, Laura wrote in *The First Four Years*.

Life did not get easier for either family. The next years saw too little rain and dropping commodity prices.

Laura and Almanzo sang, "Don't Leave the Farm Boys," during their courting days in De Smet, South Dakota. I wonder if George and Anna also sang these words:

> Come boys, I have something to tell you,
> Come near, I would whisper it low,
> You're thinking of leaving the homestead,
> Don't be in a hurry to go.
> The city has many attractions,
> But think of the vices and sins,
> When once in the vortex of fashion,
> How soon the course downward begins.
>
> *Chorus:*
> Don't be in a hurry to go!
> Don't be in a hurry to go!
> Better risk the old farm awhile longer,
> Don't be in a hurry to go!

You talk of the mines of Australia,
They're wealthy in gold without doubt,
But sh! There is gold on the farm, boys,
If only you'd shovel it out.
The mercantile trade is a hazard,
The goods are first high and then low,
Best risk the old farm a while longer,
Don't be in a hurry to go.

The great busy west has inducements,
And so has the business mart,
But wealth is not made in a day, boys,
Don't be in a hurry to start.
The bankers and brokers are wealthy,
They take in their thousand or so,
And think of the frauds and deceptions,
Don't be in a hurry to go.

The farm is the safest and surest,
The orchards are loaded today,
You're free as the air of the mountains,
And monarch of all you survey.
Best stay on the farm a while longer,
Though profits come in rather slow,
Remember you've nothing to risk, boy,
Don't be in a hurry to go.

Then came the watershed year of 1893. American optimism and exuberance turned to panic and depression. For both families, it would soon be time to go.

Eight

Dimly in my mind, I remember the expression "The Panic of 1893" from American History 101. That sounds so temporary and short-lived but, in reality, a series of events came together that year that resulted in a very serious worldwide depression. It lasted more than four years, almost a third of the duration of what we now call the Great Depression of the 1930s. My image of pretty women laughing gaily might still be appropriate for some affluent debutantes around Central Park in New York City in 1894—there are always people who are immune from hard times that hit their fellow citizens—however, that was not the daily experience for most Americans, especially those like the Swartz and Wilder families living on America's farms.

Hard times started in rural America before that terrible year of 1893. God aggravated problems for those trying to make a living from the land. In the Upper Midwest and the Great Plains, rains stopped coming for three successive years, and the winters were especially severe. The thirsty land that should be green in the spring was just dry dust. Commodity prices dropped and the inflated land prices tumbled. Banks that had loaned money based on the value of the land saw their assets depleted and consequently failed. Iowa farmers had no cash, and supplies were scarce. But many had cows, and corn still rose from the soil. So they used butter to grease the wagon wheels and burned corn for fuel, since it was cheaper and more readily available than coal. It is an understatement to say that it was not an easy time for farmers.

Laura's daughter Rose wrote vividly of that time:

> *For seven years there had been too little rain. The prairies were dust. Day after day, summer after summer, the scorching winds blew the dust and the sun was brassy in a yellow sky. Crop after crop failed. Again and again the barren land must be mortgaged, for taxes and food and next year's seed. The agony of hope ended when there was no harvest and no more credit, no money to pay interest and taxes; the banker took the land. Then the bank failed.*

The bubble burst for the rest of America in 1893. In hindsight, it is clear that the heavily leveraged economy was not built on a firm foundation. The railroads had engaged in rate wars, borrowed heavily to finance the westward expansion, and sold highly inflated stock to raise money. There were complicated monetary policy issues between the gold and silver standards that were both circulating as money. The first clear signs of trouble came in February, when the Philadelphia and Reading Railroad filed for bankruptcy. Consequently, European investors cashed in their American stocks. On April 21, 1893, the federal gold reserve limit was reached. The financial community panicked. Banks called in their loans; businesses that could not pay the loans began to fail; and banks were left with loans that were not worth the paper on which they were written. So, more banks closed their doors.

Unemployment rose amid the massive foreclosures. Tensions and unrest mounted in the country. As one chronicler of the period wrote: "*The 'heart-breaking nineties' were packed with grim facts that tried men's souls—hard times, business failures, mortgaged farms, and labor disturbances."*

Will Carleton, a popular poet of the time, wrote of the sad reality for many in his poem "Mortgage":

> We worked through spring and winter, through summer And through fall;
>
> But the mortgage worked the hardest and steadiest of them all;
> It worked on nights and Sundays, it worked each holiday;
> It settled down among us and never went away …
>
> And there came a dark day on us when the interest wasn't paid,
> And there came a sharp foreclosure and I kind o' lost my hold
> And grew weary and discouraged and the farm was cheaply sold,
> The children left and scattered, when they hardly yet were grown; …
>
> My wife, she pined and perished, an' I found myself alone,
> What she died of was a mystery, and the doctors never knew;
> But I know she died of mortgage just as well as I wanted to.

A populist movement arose. Its leaders demanded that the government provide a public works program to put people back to work. The country needed roads and bridges, and there were men who could build them. An Ohio businessman named Jacob Coxey pushed this concept and organized a group of people to march on Washington. Nicknamed the Coxey Army, a ragtag group of people started traveling from as far away as San Francisco and Washington State to join this populist revolt. They wanted a jobs bill.

Iowa farmers had a complicated reaction to this movement. Coxey's followers disrupted the lives of the people living in the states that they crossed. They seized railroad cars and made normal travel impossible. The Iowa governor tried to protect the state from the ensuing chaos and temporarily blocked the marchers at the Missouri River at Council Bluffs. But he relented and let the marchers cross the state. As the army moved toward Des Moines, Iowans gathered food and supplies to feed the marchers. But when the food supply began to run short, citizens of the Hawkeye State became less supportive. They openly worried about the sanitary conditions of the "army," as the popular tune of the day indicated:

I suppose you've heard of Coxey
And his army on the tramp;
'Tis composed of various elements,
from the worker to the scamp.
They are marching on to Washington
Our Congressmen to see;
They propose to change existing laws
to suit us all to a T.

Chorus:
Then go join Coxey's army, if you want to see the earth;
In a Pullman car you'll ride, with the doors hung on the side,
if you go join Coxey's army.

They have vowed they ne'er will wash their face
Until their journey's o'er,
And I don't think that they'll wash them then,
For they've not done it much before,
they are going to put out greenbacks
on the monthly installment plan.
If you want your share of whisky or beer,
Just follow up Coxey's band.

The Swartz family lived fifty miles from the state capital. The Des Moines papers carried detailed accounts of the Coxeyites' progress. It is not hard to imagine that my great-grandpa and his friends talked about these marchers. Perhaps some agreed with the righteousness of their cause. Others probably felt anxiety and unease. It was the first protest march on Washington, and some reported that over 10,000 marchers reached our nation's capital. They failed to persuade Congress, but in the summer of 1894, the Coxey Army dominated the news.

Not all Americans called on the government to solve their problems. Private charitable organizations tried to feed the hungry, and people planted community gardens. Other farmers tried cooperative ventures, and many joined together in a fraternal organization, the Grange, to try to raise prices by jointly selling crops. But these efforts could not change the climate. Crops still withered from lack of rain, and blizzards still came in the winter.

Dreams and hope fueled the American migration story. The bountiful frontier had drawn people to America for almost 150 years. Virgin land was there for the taking (once you got rid of the native inhabitants). Pioneers like Charles Ingalls, Almanzo Wilder, and George Swartz pushed the frontier westward.

If settlers did not find their land of milk and honey in one location, they picked up stakes and moved further west. As America sunk into a depression, there was a new reality. The U.S. Census Bureau issued the results of the 1890 Census. There was no longer a vast amount of unsettled land. The U.S. government announced that the frontier was officially closed.

However, land developers and railroads found a new dream to push, a *new* Promised Land. It was the Missouri Ozarks.

Nine

The railroads were America's first monopolies. Gilded Age fortunes were built from land granted by the government. In 1894, western railroads were faced with economic conditions that had already bankrupted their Eastern counterparts. They were eager to unload property they no longer needed. The Kansas City, Fort Scott and Memphis Railroad was no exception. Their tracks ran from Fort Scott, Kansas, into Southern Missouri, through the small towns of my parent's youth: Liberal, Lamar, Golden City in Barton County, and Lockwood in Dade County. The railroad then continued into the major city of Southwest Missouri, Springfield, in Greene County. East of Springfield sits Mansfield, in Wright County. This was where Laura and Almanzo Wilder eventually settled.

The Kansas City, Fort Scott and Memphis Railroad created a brilliant marketing campaign. The Missouri Ozarks became the "The Land of the Big Red Apple." Land around the railroad was promoted as "The last good land to be had in the 'Corn Belt' at Low Prices." No one noticed that much of the land was really not that good. There were slick posters placed in railroad cars and train depots throughout the Northern Plains and Iowa. Newspaper advertisements praised South Missouri. A book titled *Among the Ozarks, the Land of the Big Red Apples* was offered free to anyone who requested it. Promoted as "an

County Map of Missouri

Barton, Dade, Greene, and Wright Counties in South Missouri are shaded. In the northwest corner of the state is Holt, the county where my parents eventually settled and where I was raised. Boone County is the home of the University of Missouri at Columbia.

attractive and interesting book, handsomery (sic) illustrated with views of South Missouri scenery," the book promised riches from fruit farms. In De Smet, South Dakota, Laura and Almanzo eagerly read the publication. I cannot actually put the brochure in Great-Grandpa's hands, but I did find an advertisement in a Des Moines paper from 1895 offering it to "every farmer and homeseeker looking for a farm and home." J.E. Lockwood, Kansas City, Missouri, offered to mail it free to anyone who asked. Mr. Lockwood did not identify that he was an agent of the railroad.

Both the Swartz and Wilder families were persuaded. They packed up their belongings and headed south for a new life.

Rose and Carrie were both young girls when their parents made the decision to move. Laura Wilder kept a detailed diary. These daily observations during the trip to Missouri were published after her death as *On the Way Home, The Diary of a Trip from South Dakota to Mansfield, Missouri, in 1894.* She describes the world that both families saw.

Rose Wilder Lane prepared the diary for publication in 1962 and provided historical context for her family's move in a forward. Rose paints a vivid picture of the drought, depression, and economic conditions of the 1890s. She even blames Coxey's Army for disrupting railroad travel and forcing her family to travel by covered wagon, just as Laura had traveled as a child.

We know from Rose that Laura and Almanzo started out for Missouri with one hundred dollars to buy land. Theirs was a leap of faith. They would eventually settle east of Springfield, in Mansfield. The Swartz's took a different approach. In some respects, George appears to be more of a planner than Almanzo. He tried to protect his family's future by trading his Iowa farm for land in Barton County, Missouri, close to the Kansas border. I fantasize that the Wilders and Swartzes would have been on the road at the same time. I want to believe that Anna and Laura waved to each other from passing wagons.

George settled down with Anna and their three daughters in the heart of the Missouri tallgrass prairie country in Golden City. The Kansas prairie where Laura once lived in her *little house* extends into Missouri. The land rises as you move east and forms the hills known as the Missouri Ozark Mountains. The railroad publicists wrote of this land:

About one-half of Barton, Dade and Greene is smooth, beautiful prairie, with deep, productive soil, and devoted to agriculture mainly. The apple is being liberally planted and coming into successful fruiting in Barton and Dade. In Greene there are thousands of acres of full bearing orchards from which large crops of excellent fruit are shipped out west and south annually. The utility and profits of the enterprise have been so well and satisfactorily tested here that hundreds of acres are being annually planted in the country near Springfield, on and near the railroads—two trunks and their branches.

It sounds so much easier to plant apple trees and wait to pick the apples than to worry about grasshoppers eating the wheat crop. So, maybe I can cut Great-Grandpa Swartz a little slack for making what would prove to be a poor business decision, in hindsight.

Laura passed through the land where George would settle. On August 24, 1894, she wrote:

At noon we were going through Golden City, a nicer littler place. The country looks good, but judging from weeds in the gardens and fields, the people are shiftless. This is a land of many springs and clear brooks. Some of the earth is yellow and some is red. The road is stony often.

Ten-year-old Carrie did not notice the weeds. On March 13, 1964, she wrote to her granddaughters from our home in North Missouri about arriving at Golden City almost seventy years before:

When we first came to Missouri, we came to that place near Golden City. The leaves were good sized on the eleventh

day of March and we were so pleased with the country for it
was winter in Iowa ... I am still partial to South Missouri.

George must have realized that his new land was very different
than the black soil of Central Iowa. Any dreams he may have
had about *big red apple* trees in Barton County would not
materialize. In 1914, just ten years later, the U.S. Department
of Agriculture, in conjunction with the University of Missouri,
wrote:

> *Fruit growing is of very little importance in Barton County.*
> *There are usually a few apple and peach trees on each farm*
> *to supply the family needs. ... The flat prairie soils are not*
> *adapted to fruit production. The growing of truck and small*
> *fruit has not been developed on a commercial scale, though*
> *enough of each is grown to supply the home demand.*

Ten

As George and Anna became accustomed to the ways of their new land, America was entering the twentieth century. All eyes were soon on Missouri, with St. Louis taking center stage. In 1901, planning for the Louisiana Purchase Exposition began. The exposition opened in 1904 and officially celebrated the centennial of the Louisiana Purchase Treaty. Thomas Jefferson's farsighted agreement with France to purchase the American heartland was signed in 1803. This exposition became known as the St. Louis World's Fair. It was quite an extravaganza, celebrating new technology and popular culture. Electricity was just coming into its own and lit all the magnificent buildings erected for the fair.

My image of the world's fair does not come from history books, but was formed by Judy Garland singing "Meet Me in St. Louis" in the popular MGM musical by that name. The movie was made toward the end of World War II, in 1944. No matter how many times I have seen the movie, I love the story of Judy and her sisters living with their happy family in St. Louis in 1903. The budding romances of the older daughters are all threatened by their father announcing that he has been offered a lucrative position in New York. It paints a romantic picture of the times: pretty dresses, good looking beaus, music, and trolley cars. At the end of the movie, Mr. Smith announces that the family will not leave St. Louis when he realizes how much his family would be adversely affected by the move. The entire cast takes two horse-drawn buggies to the World's Fair and looks out at the grand pavilions as thousands of electric lights illuminate the fair grounds. There are weddings just over the horizon, as boyfriends presumably will become husbands after the credits roll across the screen.

Carrie, Elba, and Grace Swartz did not share this fantasy life in their home across the state. Of course, the romantic version of America depicted in the movie was not shared by all in St. Louis either. There was a growing disparity between conditions in rural and urban America. Technology that was changing the life of many in the cities had not yet reached Southwest Missouri. Like the other women in Barton County, Anna did the housework, prepared the family meals, baked bread on her wood stove, made clothes for her girls and George, cleaned them on a scrub board, and then hung the heavy wet clothes on a line to dry. It was woman's work to milk the cows, churn the butter, feed the chickens, gather the eggs, and kill and pluck the non-producing chickens. Anna also raised vegetables and canned the garden produce. Still, she somehow found the time to nurture and love George, Carrie, Elba, and Grace.

Anna passed on the art of being a farmwife to her girls. She taught them necessary skills and expected them to help with all this work. Each daughter had assigned chores. One of Carrie's assignments was to take care of the chickens. Gathering eggs sounds kind of fun, but I cringe when I realize that before you can fry chicken or cook dumplings in stock made from boiling the bird, you first have to kill it, usually by wringing its neck. This experience left a lifelong impression on my grandmother that I was not able to fully appreciate. I was a child from a small town, not a farm. Chicken came to our house from a package bought at Kreek's Grocery Store. When we passed the plate of fried chicken at our Sunday dinner, I watched as Grandma Carrie passed it on without taking a piece. She did not eat chicken.

Carrie did find time to draw during her teenage years. It is from these years that she created the drawings that I now treasure. She was quiet, creative, obviously sensitive, and from her picture taken when she was sixteen, she was very pretty too. In the picture, her hair curls charmingly around her face. But, shortly after the picture was taken, she developed a severe case of scarlet fever. This disease is marked by a red rash, a sore throat, and a high fever, usually over 101 degrees. It often hits children and is caused by a strep bacteria, the same bacteria that can result in strep throat.

Carrie Elsie Swartz at age 16

Soon, scarlet fever would cause her to lose her pretty curly hair.

Carrie Swartz drew the world that she saw.

Top: Song Birds

Middle Left: Lace Wings
and Eggs

Bottom Right: Rooster

The Poppy.

Top Left: Poppies
Top Right: Horse
Bottom Right: Kittens

Due to the miracle of antibiotics, scarlet fever is one of those serious childhood illnesses that no longer threatens our young, but it often caused death in previous times. In the Swartz house, the only treatment was to try to bring the fever down and pray. Whether by divine intervention or just good fortune, Carrie survived. But it was not without some serious consequences. It furthered her genetic predisposition for hearing problems, as the fever damaged one of her eardrums.

Equally significant for Carrie was that she lost her curly hair. Carrie's hair did grow back, but the curls were gone and it came in straight and strong. Everyone who remembers my grandmother talks about her pretty hair. Each of her granddaughters tells of watching Grandma Carrie fix her hair, her own special daily ritual. My older sister Lou Ann's memory is especially poignant, because she recalls Grandma Carrie combing her hair by the light of a kerosene lamp; Grandma's home never had electricity.

Carrie Swartz before her marriage

This small picture is the only photo I have seen of Carrie at the time of her courtship with Finn. It was sent to me by the granddaughter of Carrie's sister Elba. "Aunt Carrie Swartz" was written on the back of the photo.

I do not know if it was her quiet personality or her hearing loss that kept her from finding a husband sooner, but at twenty-six, when it seemed she was on her way to being an old maid, a much younger Finn McCluey came a courting. I have a glimpse into that courtship. I found a picture of Finn printed on a postcard. The best I can guess is that it was created around 1910. Postcards such as this were all the fashion then, perhaps the precursor to today's selfies. It is addressed to Miss Carrie Swartz. Finn is serious in the picture, as it was not yet appropriate to smile for the camera. He is dressed in a shiny shirt, and his hat sits cocked to one side. I find the man who would become my grandfather cute and a little appealing. But, he also looks very young, still someplace between a boy and a man.

Finn McCluey, circa 1910

Finn printed his photo on a postcard and addressed it to Miss Carrie Swartz, the precursor of today's selfies.

I am struck by Carrie's age because both my mother and I also married later than was the norm at the time, Mom at twenty-eight and me at thirty-four. As they said in Carrie's time, none of us were spring chickens! Even so, the men we chose to marry influenced much of the rest of our lives. Each came to marriage from another family, with their own traditions and stories. In spite of the biblical injunction that a man shall leave his father and his mother and cleave unto his wife, no man completely leaves his family and his childhood behind. Inevitably, early life experiences affect how a man treats his wife and children.

Carrie had had the benefit of two loving parents, George and Anna. But Finn's family experience was very different. That difference had a significant effect on Carrie's subsequent life.

Wait Until the Darkness Is Over

Eleven

My memories of Finn McCluey are from 1959, the last year of his life.

The small home that my parents rented for my grandparents was located across from the Oregon Christian Church, just down the block from my dad's medical office. It was the first time that my grandparents lived in a house that had electricity. The black and white TV screen was in a boxed cabinet and sat in the center of my grandparents' living room. Grandpa was glued to the TV during that year. The fifties version of America's story, a western, always seemed to be playing on it. He had loved westerns since he first heard a Zane Grey story as a boy. Finn McCluey had no trouble finding a show on television that featured cowboys, saloons, and six shooters. The top four rated television shows that year were all westerns, with *Gunsmoke* leading the pack.

Grandpa McCluey sat close to the television screen, always holding a cigarette up to his mouth. It seemed as soon as he finished one cigarette, he began the ritual of preparing his next one. He rolled his own, tapping out the dried leaves from a can labelled Country Gentlemen Tobacco onto the lightweight paper. He used his moist tongue to seal the paper after he formed it into a cigarette. Then, too often, his thin body was racked by coughing. Increasingly, emphysema was choking off the ability of his lungs to process the oxygen his thin body so desperately needed.

Still, Grandpa paid attention to me and teased me. I knew that I was always welcome at my grandparents' and often stopped by after school. Grandma was there in the background, but it is my grandfather that I remember from that year. Grandpa gave me my afternoon snack, usually consisting of store bought cookies. Grandpa McCluey is more than a two-dimensional figure to me because, like his daughters, I loved him. Children do not always see the realities of life that surround them, but they do recognize when they are loved. In turn, they give love back.

My grandparents' house that year became my refuge. Down the street in my dad's office, the world was beginning to spin out of control for my parents. Although it may have been obvious to an observer that my grandfather was in the last year of his life, the long lines of patients waiting to see Doc Sweaney had not yet realized that my father would also soon die. But down deep, my mother probably knew. Life in my father's world was increasingly intense, and Dad's exhaustion and health issues were hard for my mother to continue to ignore. She was becoming anxious as she tried to cope with the realities of the situation. My mother had very little time to give to a small brown-eyed little girl of seven who was craving attention.

Most of my grandfather's life had already been lived before he was moved by his daughter to his last home. My Aunt Avis left a written account of her childhood. When I read his youngest daughter's words, it was hard for me not to be angry at Finn McCluey and the way he treated his wife, Carrie. There was never physical abuse in Aunt Avis's narrative, but you have to wonder if Grandpa had a drinking problem. In the way of his Scots-Irish people, he clung fiercely to his independence, perhaps unwisely so. And a McCluey could nurse a grudge with the best of them. Any objective outsider reading of the early years of his adult life and marriage would have to judge him, at the very least, as irresponsible and immature. My aunt later wrote of her father:

> *With all of Dad's faults, he was a loveable dad, and we wouldn't have traded him for any other. Dad taught us to respect others regardless of color, creed, rich or poor. He was honest and didn't believe in cheating people.*

Daughters may often be blind to the flaws of their fathers, but their mothers often are not. Carrie McCluey had wisdom about life that her second daughter, Iris, inherited. She once told her three daughters that "your father is irresponsible because he did not have a mother to guide him."

Twelve

My Grandpa Finn McCluey's mother died when he was just a toddler. Her name was Sarah Harwell McCluey. She spent her adult life having babies.

I was twelve when my mother told me the story of her McCluey grandparents. I was still lost in my romantic fantasies of Laura and Almanzo from the *Little House* books. The story of Bob McCluey and Sarah Harwell somehow fed those fantasies. I loved her name. I told myself that if I ever had a little girl, I would name her Sarah Harwell. But Robert and Sarah McCluey's life was not the "happily-ever-after story" of a twelve-year-old's dreams.

Like my own life, my grandfather's was affected by a parent who died too young. Both of our childhoods were changed by the disorder that comes with grief. The person that we became was in no small part molded by that reality. I am not sure that Bob McCluey, my great-grandfather, ever truly recovered from losing his wife. It was not that it was the first time that he experienced death; after all, he had seen boys die during the Siege of Vicksburg in America's Civil War. But he was not equipped to deal with the realities of losing his beloved wife and raising eight children by himself. I have learned that you should never judge how someone else internalizes life events. However, I do know that how they do so affects those around them, especially children.

Sarah Harwell was eighteen when she caught Bob McCluey's eyes at a church social in 1870. In the way of soldiers returning from battle, Bob McCluey was ready to get married. Bob had come home from war four years earlier and was ready to settle down on the family land. McCluey land was in Dade County, just across the line from Barton County, and less than ten miles from where George and Anna Swartz later settled. It was a sizable piece of property—a Section of Land, the surveyor term for 640 acres. He hauled lumber from Springfield with an ox team and built a house on the north side of his property. He had enlisted in the Union Army in Springfield in 1862 and fought with the Missouri's 6th Volunteer Regiment. He later told his granddaughter Iris, "It was my duty to help put down the Rebellion." It seemed amazing to me that my mother had clear memories of a man who had fought in the Civil War.

The young couple was surrounded by people who shared their faith and their way of life. The area of Dade County called Old Sylvania was settled by Scots-Irish, who migrated to Missouri by way of Pennsylvania. When Bob was a boy, his father, Hugh, was sent by the Great Homestead Mining Company out of Pittsburgh to start a coal mining center in South Missouri. But the coal mined in the McCluey mines never lived up to the coal in Pennsylvania and, increasingly, the McClueys turned their attention to farming. Hugh and his wife, Martha, came to America as part of the great migration from the Ulster-Scots Plantation of Northern Ireland. They fit many of the stereotypes of America's Scots-Irish, including strong religious convictions, a fierce independent streak, and incredible distrust of centralized authority.

Bob's mother, Martha, took little Finn home with her after her daughter-in-law's funeral. I hope that his grandmother was able to give the little boy some gentleness, some love. But that is not the image of Martha McCluey that has come down through family stories. Instead, I have a picture of a stern, devoutly religious woman. In her home, the Sabbath was honored from sundown Saturday evening until sundown on Sunday. No work was to be done during that time. Before the Sabbath began on Saturday, all wood was chopped and brought into the house, kerosene lamps were trimmed, and all meals were prepared. The Sabbath was a day of rest and consecration. If visitors happened by the house on a Sunday, Martha asked about the health of their family and then handed them a Bible to read.

While Finn was living with his Grandmother, Bob McCluey's family suffered another death. Finn's ten-year-old brother Lewis was taken by one of those many illnesses that brought death to young children in the late nineteenth century. In 1892, just two years after Sarah's death, Bob again opened the family Bible and turned to those pages following the Old Testament. This time, with a pain that no parent ever wants to feel, Bob wrote his son's name and the date he died. Then, recalling the biblical story of King David and his son Absalom, my great-grandfather added, "*O my son Lewis, my son, my son, would God I had died for thee.*"

The McCluey experience was far from unusual. In 1900, half of young people had at least one parent die before they reached age twenty-one. If a mother had four children, there was a fifty percent chance that one of these children would die before the age of five. Lewis had beaten the odds by living until he was ten.

When Finn was six, his grandmother announced that he was now old enough to live in his father's home. The one daughter, Maud, was married by then so Finn returned to an all-male household that was still processing the loss of both Sarah and Lewis.

Finn at age 6

Until this point, Finn was clothed in dresses, the style for little boys during the late nineteenth century. When he turned six, his grandmother dressed him as a boy and sent him home to live with his father.

Bob McCluey raised his sons alone without a woman's assistance. He too often fulfilled the image that people carry about the Ozark Mountains. He feuded with neighbors and was slow to let go of a perceived slight. Bob McCluey had a fight with Finn's third-grade teacher. No one remembers what angered Bob, but he pulled the little boy out of the school. Finn never had any formal education beyond that point. Finn was naturally gifted in *figures*, but his reading stayed at a grade school level for the rest of his life.

Thirteen

When Finn came of age, his father gave him a hundred acres on the south side of McCluey land to farm. Finn built a small house for Carrie on this land and covered it with tar paper. I was only six the last time I saw the McCluey homestead. I vaguely recall kerosene lamps and having to use an outhouse. My older cousins Marilyn and Ruth gave me their memories. They both painted similar pictures of the home where Carrie and Finn raised their daughters.

The original house only had four rooms: a dining room, living room, and two bedrooms. Later, Finn added a kitchen and a back porch. Two large butter churns were kept on this porch. Carrie, of course, made the butter after the cows were milked. Later, it was her daughters' responsibility to milk the cows, but until the girls were old enough, this duty fell to the woman of the house. Above the sill of the door were two old mining lanterns, a testimony to the McCluey coal mining heritage.

Two large galvanized tubs took up much of the remaining space on the small porch. It was at these tubs that Carrie hand-washed her family's clothes using a scrub board. She then hung the heavy wet clothes out on a line to dry. She heated heavy irons on the stove and used them to press out any wrinkles. Except for the heavy overalls that Finn lived in, all the other clothes were handmade by Carrie. It was hard work just to make sure they were clean.

The kitchen had a wood cook stove. It was here that Carrie made the meals for her family. The family depended on Carrie's garden for most of the food during the summer. In the winter, food came from the mason jars Carrie filled during August and September. Dishes were stored in a pie cabinet that sat against one wall. On the top right-hand corner of the cabinet, Carrie always kept a word list, where she listed words with their meanings. It was a list that seemed to always be growing, as she found a continuing supply of new words in newspapers and books, especially from her Bible commentary.

The small work table in the room always had a newspaper on it. Carrie read it when she could take a break from her chores. The newspaper was usually yellowed with age before Carrie had time to read it all and replace it with another. In the dining room, a round wooden oak table was surrounded by four heavy wooden chairs. An old-fashioned buffet stood against the wall. In the living room was Finn's chair. It was reserved for him. Later, the family had a radio powered by batteries. It and the *Kansas City Star* were the family's link to the outside world.

The smaller bedroom was shared by the daughters who came later. The larger of the two bedrooms was reserved for Finn and Carrie. In it was a small desk where Robert McCluey's picture was featured prominently. The iron bedstead took up most of the small room. Magazines and newspapers were stacked in the corner of the room. They almost reached to the ceiling. Perhaps Carrie always hoped there would be time to return to them and read them again and again. But her life was too busy to lend itself to casual reading.

The small house didn't offer much beauty, but Carrie always kept house plants. They did well and added green and perhaps some red to the living room. However, it is the color *brown* that I think of when I recall my grandparents' house and land. It is not a rich velvet brown, but rather a light brown of loose dirt and dust. Grandma Carrie did try to add some beauty to the sparse landscape. Honeysuckle and wild roses surrounded the tarpaper. The outside flowers grew around the house, willy-nilly, in their own manner. Carrie never let Finn prune them.

McCluey land was not without its appeal. When there was rain, the land held a certain kind of beauty. Over on Prairie Hill, the natural grasses had not yet been disturbed and they still blew in the wind. And in the hollows, wild strawberries and blackberries flourished. And close to their vines, there were wildflowers. Each one carried a lyrical name assigned to it by previous Ozark generations. My mother knew the petals by these given names, such as Blue Aster, Wild Sweet William, Queen Anne's Lace, or Black-eyed Susan. And there were songbirds in the trees.

Life was not easy. The new world of technological change showcased in St. Louis just a few years earlier at the fair had not yet made its way to the Ozark foothills. Finn and Carrie settled into a pattern of married life that was not very different than earlier generations who had lived on McCluey land. Their small home, like most others in rural Southwest Missouri, did not benefit from new conveniences such as indoor plumbing and electricity that were making life easier for many in America's cities.

Since her hearing loss increased her natural tendency for introversion, Carrie was perhaps just a little more reclusive than many of her neighbors. She performed all the myriad tasks associated with "women's work." Finn worked the fields and still sometimes dug coal out of the McCluey mines. They had roles that were governed by their culture and society. But stories from my Aunt Avis make it hard for me not to be irritated at my grandfather:

> *When Dad went to the field, he had no sense of time. I guess he came home when his stomach told him it was time to eat. When he came home, he expected his dinner to be on the table, hot and ready to eat. Mama would watch for him to come across the pasture, and then she would hurry with dinner.*

Finn loved to barter and make deals with the other men in the area. He didn't have much cash in his pocket, but he used his cows to trade for other items. Carrie, and later his daughters, never knew how many cows they would find to milk. Sometimes cows disappeared, given to another farmer as part of a deal, while at other times a new cow just appeared as a result of one of Finn's trades.

Carrie did not leave the isolated house very much. She sent Finn to town ten miles away for goods and groceries. Finn seemed to enjoy these outings. It was fun to talk and joke with other men. Perhaps he had just a little too much fun because he could forget that he had a home with a waiting wife. Avis remembered:

> *Mama often went to the door and looked out. With a worried look in her eyes, she would say, "I wonder what has happened to your dad?" Then she would go back, taking care of her jelly on the stove.*

Sometimes, it was the next day before Finn returned and, then, without the list of items that he was to buy. My aunt remembered another story that makes my heart ache for Grandma Carrie:

> *Like most country schools in those days, there was a carry-in dinner for the last day of school. Mama wrote a list of items she expected Dad to get in town for the school dinner. Dad showed up after the dinner the next day. Mama didn't have anything to take to the dinner.*

Carrie did not have much time in those years for leisure activities. She was an adult with responsibilities. There is still evidence of the things that she loved from her drawings. She always seemed to have a litter of cute kittens that she fed with leftover milk from the cows. She had her houseplants and flowers. But she was now a woman, and as the apostle Paul said, she had to "put away childish things." There was no time for drawing.

Never again did Carrie pick up a pencil or pen and create pretty pictures.

Fourteen

I found a small yellowed membership card made out in Carrie McCluey's name in a box of old family papers. It was for the Women's Christian Temperance Union.

Women of my generation are quick to praise the women activists of the early twentieth century. We admire the women in the cities who combatted poverty by starting settlement houses and others who worked to put new child labor laws on the books. The suffragettes who chained themselves to the White House fence and marched with banners across their chest in order to secure the vote are feminist icons. But we lampoon the temperance movement. Carrie Nation, the ax wielding, saloon smashing opponent of demon rum, is a caricature.

I can understand why my grandmother and women like her were drawn to this movement. Temperance was a cause that affected them personally. Alcohol consumption was a serious social issue in those early decades of the twentieth century. Americans were spending over a billion dollars on alcoholic beverages each year, compared with $900 million on meat and less than $200 million on public education. The movement's leaders linked alcoholism with spousal abuse, family neglect, and chronic unemployment.

The Women's Christian Temperance Union (WCTU) grew out of the Woman's Crusade of the winter of 1873-1874. In Upstate New York, a group of women were moved after listening to a lecture on the dangers of alcohol. *"Normally quiet housewives dropped to their knees in pray-ins in local saloons and demanded that the sale of liquor be stopped."* These women went beyond this "revival" experience and organized to fight for change. They began to understand that they had power by standing together. Within three months after this New York lecture, they had driven liquor out of two hundred fifty communities.

The WCTU promoted the concept that "all reform was interconnected and that social problems could not be separated." The emphasis on abstaining from alcohol and other drugs distinguished it from other activists groups, but it stood alongside the suffragettes as women fought for social change. Railing against saloons was as much a political activity as a social one, since most local political meetings were held in saloons, from which women were excluded.

The WCTU grew out of the realities of the times. Women not only did not have the right to vote, but in most states they had no control over their property or rights in divorce proceedings. Under the leadership of Frances Willard, the organization became one of the largest and most influential women's groups of the late nineteenth century. The fight for temperance became intertwined with other social movements of the time, such as changing labor laws, prison reform, and, most importantly, the movement to gain women the right to vote. After Willard's death in 1898, there was a split in the organization and many of the WCTU leaders distanced themselves from feminists who used militant tactics to secure the vote.

In Missouri, the WCTU worked locally to change county and municipal laws incrementally. They created "dry" counties out of previously "wet" ones. (A wet county allowed the sale of alcohol, dry counties did not.) By 1910, they turned Dade County dry, and by 1916, the rest of the Ozarks followed. Missouri was declared a dry state even before the Eighteenth Amendment to the United States Constitution took effect on January 16, 1920. This amendment declared that in the United States it was illegal to produce, transport or sale alcohol although it was still legal to consume it. It was ratified six months before the ratification of the Nineteenth Amendment, giving women the right to vote. By that year, the WCTU was the largest woman's organization in Missouri. An official *History of Missouri*, published in 1920, noted, "The educational work of WCTU has had an influence which no one can measure."

Herbert Hoover called prohibition a "noble experiment," but it was doomed to fail. It was credited with the rise of crime and violence in Chicago and other American cities. In only thirteen years, the amendment to prohibit alcohol was repealed through another constitutional amendment, but this experiment helped to create an enduring image of the Missouri Ozarks as a land full of stills and moonshiners.

I do not know where and when my grandmother joined the WCTU. It was always my impression that she did not leave the house to socialize. I cannot picture her as any kind of an activist. But she was moved to join this cause. In doing so, I think she was making a statement. She wanted her daughters and granddaughters to live in a different world.

Fifteen

Carrie was a wife for a little over two years before she became a mother. By then, she was thirty. She had put aside her drawings, but she did not completely bury her creative side; it came out in the names that she gave to her daughters. Gwendolyn Mae came along first, in 1914. Carrie's middle child, my mother, Iris Myrtle, was born in 1918. And four years later, Avis Marie joined the family.

There was another little girl. Her name was Winnifred June. She was Carrie's second baby, born between my Aunt Gwen and my mother. She lived for two days. They buried her in a small grave, with only a wooden marker. My stoic grandmother kept her emotions buried inside her, but my cousin Ruth remembers tears in Grandma Carrie's eyes years later when she could not find Winnifred June's grave. The wooden marker had disappeared.

It was another two decades before scientists discovered why second babies sometimes died. There was a pattern, small but still significant, that some mothers had a normal first birth, and then her second baby was stillborn or died shortly afterwards. In 1937, scientists discovered that red blood cells in some individuals were different from those of others. Blood types were more complicated than originally believed. Some people were missing something that would be called the Rh factor, named for the blood of the Rhesus monkey. It was a genetic condition that ran in some families. Three years later, scientists linked this discovery to the death of some newborns.

Both my mother and her mother did not have Rh proteins in their blood and, therefore, were Rh negative. Like the majority of people, Finn McCluey and my father were Rh positive. I can only assume that, like me, Winnifred June followed the pattern that babies born to an Rh negative mother and an Rh positive father are Rh positive. This condition was not a problem when Aunt Gwen or Lou Ann, my older sister, were born. In the first pregnancy, mothers do not yet have antibodies to fight off the incompatibilities in blood types. These antibodies, the body's way of responding to the invasion of the foreign blood type, are created during the first pregnancy; however, with Winnifred June's and my birth, our mother's bodies recognized the Rh proteins in our blood as foreign. Their immune system attacked these cells. By the time I was born in 1952, the medical profession realized the danger. Doctors responded by giving me a blood transfusion and I survived. In 2014, my niece who has Rh negative blood was given antibodies during her pregnancy to protect her unborn baby. Nothing was available to protect little Winnifred June.

Iris and Avis grew to become best friends. They walked hand-in-hand to the one-room Stone School, and on the way they found pretty stones in the rocky soil. In that world of make-believe that only children can inhabit, they were sometimes joined by their fantasy little sister, Winnifred June, who lived in heaven with the angels. Although they never knew this baby sister, she was very real to them.

Students at Stone School, circa 1932

Iris McCluey can be seen in the top row. Her face is partially blocked by the boy in front of her.

During the summer months, when there was no school, they picked blackberries and brought wildflower bouquets home to their mother. They watched Carrie turn the berries into jellies and pies. As Carrie had done with her mother, Anna, Iris and Avis helped their mother make sauerkraut, and waited for days as the cabbage fermented in the big stoneware crock, the smell permeating the small house. They mastered the Pennsylvania Dutch art of mixing eggs and flour together, rolling out the mixture onto a floured surface, and cutting it with a knife to form thin noodles, and then they learned to judge just the right time to drop the noodles into the hot chicken or beef broth.

After supper, Carrie sat with her mending basket in her lap. Her stiches were always neat and tidy. Seldom in her life did she have a sewing machine, so she made her daughter's dresses completely by hand. Carrie drew her own patterns on paper, using ideas inspired by Sears and Roebuck catalogues. Using scrap material for her clever designs, she created new dresses for her daughters. Finn somehow always managed to have a big hole in one of his socks. Carrie put a cup inside the sock to mimic Finn's ankle, and with precise stitches, she darned the sock. Her daughter Avis once said that her mother's darning was like a piece of artwork.

When the work for the day was done, the family sat in the living room together and Carrie read aloud their favorite books: Dickens' *David Copperfield,* tales from Zane Grey about the American West for Finn, and Harold Bell Wright's description of life in the Missouri Ozarks in *Shepherd of the Hills.* The nightly ritual concluded with Carrie reading a chapter from the Bible, and then the family knelt down to say the Lord's Prayer. Finn lowered the wick of the kerosene lamp, and Iris and Avis were sent to the bed that they shared.

At night, the wind blew right through the tarpaper, and there were never enough covers to keep out the cold. The two little girls cuddled together, sharing their warmth. Before they closed their eyes to sleep, Iris and Avis talked about the day's adventures and whispered about the baby sister with the pretty name. Years later, they told their daughters about Winnifred June, the little baby who did not make it.

Sixteen

"The only thing we have to fear is fear itself." Franklin Delano Roosevelt proclaimed these words in his first inaugural address in 1933. They were not a great comfort to Finn McCluey, listening to them on his battery-powered radio. The words were too late. For fear had already embraced Finn and his family. By the time the New Deal officially started, fear was palpable in that small tarpapered house. The McCluey land was heavily mortgaged, and the next bank payment was always looming. Finn worried constantly that next month he might not be able to scrape up enough to keep the bank from seizing the McCluey land.

Finn and Carrie McCluey, circa 1934

You can see on their faces the realities of hard times for the McCluey family.

The Hungry Years is how historian T.H. Watkins refers to the Great Depression. For the McCluey girls coming of age, it was an apt description. There was not much to eat during the winter months. Hard times started for rural America long before the stock market crashed on Black Friday in October 1929. The country lyrics, "Well, somebody told us Wall Street fell, but we were so poor that we couldn't tell" would have resonated with Finn.

It all started with the First World War. The "War to end all Wars" brought death and destruction to Europe. But it also brought prosperity, albeit short lived, to American farmers. European farmers were drafted to fight, leaving their fields fallow. War-ravaged Europe needed food, and American farmers could raise it in abundance so there was a market for all that our farmers grew. The good old law of supply and demand kicked in and American commodity prices went through the roof. Farmers reacted by expanding and buying new equipment to meet the demand. Banks were more than happy to fuel this expansion by offering loans with land as collateral.

When America entered the war in 1917, our government policies further encouraged production with artificial price supports. Finn and other farmers were even given deferments from the draft. Finn bought into the concept. He could borrow to buy seed and cattle with McCluey land as collateral. Bank payments could be made easily in the fall when crops came in and cattle went to market. Even on the poor soil of Southwest Missouri, a farmer prospered. Then the war ended.

At first, Europe still needed our products. But in 1920, the world economy took a nosedive and farm prices plummeted. This economic downturn was fairly short-lived, and by 1922, good times came back to urban America. As long as you were not trying to make a living from the land, the Roaring Twenties were an exuberant, prosperous time. However, Finn McCluey and many of his fellow farmers never recovered from this downturn. Finn felt he had no choice but to borrow more money to just stay afloat. Before the thirties were over, he was carrying three mortgages on his land.

In rural America, one depression just flowed into the next. Many would live a hardscrabble life for two decades. In 1929, the annual income per person of people living on farms was only $273 dollars, while the average for most Americans was $750. In 1930, God made matters worse in farm country. He stopped sending rain, and the dry, thirsty soil cracked in the hot Missouri sun. It was the first of the drought years. Things went from bad to worse for the McClueys that year. Finn hurt his knee and could not work for months. The family called it "miner's knee," a result of years of working in the McCluey mines. The swollen knee was a gruesome sight. The local doctor had to make several house calls to drain the yellow pus from the infection. The family was almost at a breaking point. Now, in addition to the mortgage, there were doctor bills to be paid and no money for either one.

Small kindnesses from neighbors helped them get through the dark days though. One nice lady stopped by and picked up the family's dirty clothes. She had a new-fangled washing machine. She said it would be much more efficient than Carrie's washboard, and she returned the clean clothes the next day. There was not much food on the table during that time. The cows were still producing milk, but there was little meat for the table. Another neighbor dropped off a basket of turnips. Carrie mashed them with a little milk. They tasted like a delicacy to her children. And the banker agreed to work with Finn. He had plenty of land to foreclose. Anyway, what good would the McCluey land really be to the bank?

Finn McCluey was a proud Republican. He had voted for Herbert Hoover. Hoover was hailed as the Great Humanitarian after leading a campaign to feed Europeans after World War I. There was great optimism in the country when he became President in January of 1929, but before the year was over, the stock market crashed. Hoover referred to the economic crisis as a *depression*. Historians believe that the president thought this term was less alarming than the term *panic*, used previously to describe downturns in the economy. In no time at all, the widely recognized humanitarian was painted as a callous and unfeeling man. The people wanted a strong leader who was willing to try new policies to save them. This they found in a New York patrician. Franklin Delano Roosevelt had bold ideas to rescue the desperate people and who offered a New Deal for America.

The New Dealers set out to raise commodity prices to their 1914 level by limiting their supply. They began the practice of paying farmers not to grow certain products to reduce the surplus that had developed. The administration did not just discourage further planting, but they actually paid people to plow under crops already in the ground. It may have seemed like sound economic theory, but in a land full of hungry people, the sight of destroying potential food did not sit well with many. The outcry grew louder when the government slaughtered little pigs to keep them from growing up to be fat hogs, thus hoping to raise prices. Bacon, ham, and pork chops would have tasted awfully good to most Americans in 1933. The large numbers of pigs overwhelmed meat packers in Midwestern cities, including Kansas City and St. Joseph, Missouri. The meat byproducts that could not be stored or sold were dumped in the Missouri River. There were reports of carcasses with meat still on them floating down stream. It was a public relations nightmare at the very least.

The government set out to put Americans to work through a massive public works program. A Civilian Conservation Camp (CCC) was built just thirty-five miles away in Mt. Vernon, Missouri. Men and boys from Dade County were put to work in this military-style program. The Works Progress Administration (WPA) soon recruited men to build a city hall and auditorium in nearby Neosho. Finn wanted no part of these government programs. He had McCluey land and, above all else, his fierce pride. But he persevered, praying that good times would soon come. He worked hard, took what was owed him, but never wanted charity. In his mind, the New Deal polices amounted to government handouts. The Scots-Irish had always been suspicious of centralized authority. Roosevelts's big government policies went against his grain. He was not alone in these sentiments.

Over in Mansfield, Laura and Almanzo Wilder were also vehemently opposed to the New Deal. They were politically active in Republican politics. In fact, Rose Wilder Lane, their only child, later became one of the founders of America's Libertarian Party and left her papers to the Herbert Hoover Presidential Library. She would have found a kindred spirit in Finn McCluey. Rose shared a story regarding Almanzo and a government man, retold by John E. Miller in his book *Becoming Laura Ingalls Wilder, the Woman behind the Legend*:

> *One day while he was plowing with old Buck, his thirty-year-old Morgan, a young agent from the Department of Agriculture parked alongside the road and walked in the field to ask some questions about his farm operation. When*

he informed Almanzo that federal regulations prohibited him from planting more than two acres of oats, the farmer retorted that if the fellow did not immediately leave his property, he was going to get his shotgun. The agent, who was writing this down, offered Almanzo an opportunity to change his words for the record. At that point the old man made his meaning perfectly clear, in Rose's telling of the story. He said, "God damn you, you get to hell off my land and you do it now. I'll plant whatever I damn please on my own farm, and if you're on it when I get to my gun, by God I'll fill you with buckshot.

The Wilders had their fair share of challenges since moving to Missouri. "My life has mostly been disappointments," Almanzo told his daughter. Rose later wrote of the poverty of her teenage years. She left Missouri as soon as she could for adventures in San Francisco and Europe. She found some acclaim as an author, and her stories appeared in popular magazines. She even wrote a rather condescending book about small town life based on her memories of Mansfield. Rose's success encouraged her mother. Soon, Laura was able to supplement her family's income through her own writing.

Before she became the beloved children's author, Mrs. A.J. Wilder's columns were featured in the magazine *Missouri Ruralist* during the twenties. Her words bordered on the inspirational in a series titled "As a Farm Woman Thinks." She offered farm women concrete tips based on her own experience, such as "Economy in Egg Production." This subject had a special place in Laura's heart. One of her neighbors paid her the ultimate compliment: "She gets eggs in the winter when none of her neighbors gets them." The publication was popular in Southwest Missouri. It is highly likely that it found its way to Finn and Carrie's home. Perhaps copies of the *Missouri Ruralist* were stacked with the other newspapers and magazines in their bedroom, waiting for Carrie to find the time to absorb Laura's advice.

As the economic conditions worsened, it became more difficult for Rose to sell her stories to magazines. She returned to Missouri. Looking for new markets for their writing, Rose encouraged her mother to write stories of her life. Publishers were not interested in Laura's autobiography as a pioneer girl, but an editor encouraged her to rewrite her stories, aiming them at a young audience. In 1932, her first children's book, *Little House in the Big Woods*, was released. It brought praise and cries for more stories. By 1943, seven more *Little House* books were on shelves throughout the world.

Laura Ingalls Wilder wrote America's mythic story with her family as the central characters. It is the story of people searching for that piece of land that they could call home. Her characters are named Charles and Caroline Ingalls, but so many of us can substitute our family's names in the story. She wrote of a childhood in Wisconsin, Kansas, Minnesota, and South Dakota. But the books were born during hard times in the Ozark Mountains of Missouri during the Great Depression. Laura and Almanzo Wilder's migration story ended in Southern Missouri. Hugh, Martha, and Bob McCluey also found land to call their own there. They passed that land onto Finn.

Anna Swartz's story did not end there. Her journey would continue in a loaded down Model T.

Seventeen

"I could hear the thirsty cows bleating. They wanted water. But no one had any water that summer." Iris McCluey was sixteen the summer of 1934. Those sounds haunted her for the rest of her life.

It was not just the lack of water that caused farmers west of the Mississippi to shake their fists at the heavens that year. The drought came with blistering heat. The year 1934 went down in the books as the hottest year on record for the Midwest. It was before air conditioning, and people just baked. In Kansas City, the heat was too unbearable to work, and the stockyard workers went on strike. With no people to process the cows, the livestock was shot. In St. Louis, the temperature reached at least a hundred degrees for twenty-nine days; four hundred twenty people died.

Sadly, it was not an isolated summer drought in 1934. Drought conditions would continue through the summer of 1936 resulting in the hottest day on record for Kansas City. On August 14, the thermometer registered one hundred thirteen. That year proved even more deadly for St. Louis than 1934, for four hundred seventy-nine people died from the heat, including twenty-nine children. There were reports in St. Louis that the heat was "blazing enough to melt tar rooftops." Crowded with heatstroke victims, hospitals set up beds in the hallways. Patients had to wait to be doused with ice-filled buckets, and infants were cooled by fans blowing across stacks of ice. The high temperatures in the summer of 1936 remain the most extreme in North American history.

McCluey land suffered with this heat and drought. When Finn tried to pick up a handful of dirt, it just blew away. There was no moisture or grass to hold the soil together. It joined the dust already in the air, blowing east from Kansas and Oklahoma. In the house, Carrie turned all the glasses upside down in the cabinet and covered the plates with a dishtowel to keep the dust out. The heavens did not send rain, but insects and grasshoppers swarmed. In Southern Missouri, an infestation of worms ate any plant that actually made it up through the dry soil. It seemed to the God-fearing that they were experiencing the plagues that had been visited on Pharaoh. It is no wonder that those who fled from the dry dust would soon be called *exodusters*.

Finn, Carrie, and their daughters did not flee. They stayed. The land was his destiny. His house was not much, and the bank owned it as much as he did. Finn had been born on that land. His grandparents had settled there before the Civil War. His roots were buried someplace deep down under that cracked soil. The tree that his father had planted to honor his mother, Sarah, stood proud, marking the beginning of McCluey land. But it was a different story for his mother-in-law, Anna.

Anna had no ties to the land. Her husband, George, had been gone for a decade, having died in 1924. Missouri was just one long stop on her journey that had started years ago in Pennsylvania, with that stopover in Iowa, where her girls were born and she buried little Lester. They left that good land when it turned dry. Hard times in 1894 had driven them from Iowa to South Missouri, hopeful of apple trees and new possibilities. So, when her youngest daughter, Grace, and her husband, Ben McKenna, started talking about picking up stakes and moving, it sounded like an echo from the past. Grace and Ben heard there were jobs in California, and since there was nothing but dry, cracked soil and heat in Southwest Missouri, Anna agreed to go with them, and Carrie said goodbye to the mother she would never see again.

It was easy for Anna, Grace, and Ben to catch the road westward. Route 66 was just a hop, skip, and a jump from their home. The two-lane highway crossed into Oklahoma just on the other side of Joplin, Missouri. They found it crowded with Model Ts loaded down with possessions and people whose faces bore the look of poverty, hunger, and desperation. By the end of the decade, there would be over a million people who escaped to California on that legendary American highway. By the time they arrived in California, they were all called Okies. It did not matter if many of them came from Kansas, Nebraska, and Missouri—not just Oklahoma. Most did not find the jobs, dignity, or future they had hoped for in California; instead, they faced poverty and an increasing sense of helplessness that festered in migrant camps.

These camps gave us two of our enduring images of the Great Depression. John Steinbeck's novel, *The Grapes of Wrath* immortalized the Joad family and the personal cost of the Great Depression. The book endures and is required reading in high school and college literature classes. However, it is a photograph taken in the migrant camps that became the face of the Great Depression.

Dorothea Lange was sent by the Farm Security Administration to photograph the migrants in California. The administration was part of the collection of New Deal agencies established to address the farming crisis and rural poverty. The New Dealers found many ways to put people to work, including offering paying jobs to writers, artists, and photographers. Dorothea Lange was one of them. In 1936, she arrived in California and visited a campsite full of families who could find no work. There was nothing to pick since an early freeze had destroyed the pea crop. Lange took six pictures that day. One of them, *Migrant Mother*, is now the iconic image of the Great Depression.

My mother wrote to her Aunt Grace and Uncle Ben until Grace died in 1965. Before she gave family news, Iris McCluey Sweaney always described the weather. It is how she started all her letters. Grace understood; weather mattered. Too little rain could turn the soil to dust and too much rain could cause rivers to rise and fields to flood. Clouds could turn into black funnels in a moment, destroying buildings with their twisting winds. In winter, my mother reported on the ice and snow, or the lack thereof. And if it were summer, she always wrote of her garden and told how the green beans and tomatoes were faring.

Although the oldest of George and Anna's daughters, Carrie outlived the rest of her family. She died in 1968. Her mother, Anna, had passed on in the early 1940s, and her middle sister, Elba, died in 1954. The Swartz name did not live on through a son. But George's family represents something very American. It is the search for a place to live in dignity and to fulfill a dream.

In the year Grandma Carrie died, many Americans were still searching for such a land. We were torn apart that year by violence and bloodshed, with a war in Southeast Asia and a civil rights struggle on the home front. And two of our great dreamers, Martin Luther King Jr. and Bobby Kennedy, were assassinated.

It was the year I turned sixteen. The hot Missouri sun blazed down on my mother's garden that summer. She made me save my bathwater. I helped her dip pitchers into the tub and carried them filled with water to her garden. There, I poured them on her thirsty vegetables. I questioned her about the need to perform this ritual; after all, our neighbor was watering his garden with a hose attached to a spigot on the side of his house. She reminded me of the year that she turned my age. Then, as if she were hearing the cows bleating again, my mother said, "You never waste water."

Eighteen

Hard times continued after the dust storms subsided. Most Americans, including the McClueys, did not feel financially secure until the next decade. For prosperity to return to America, it would take the Japanese attack on Pearl Harbor in 1941 and the resulting war mobilization. In Finn and Carrie's home, there was no money for anything but the bare essentials. So their oldest daughter, Gwen, left home early, dropping out of school to take odd jobs. However, Iris and Avis McCluey were determined to go to high school. It was not easy.

During their grade school years, the two girls walked together to the one-room Stone School, but walking for Iris and Avis was now out of the question since the high school was eleven miles away in Lockwood. Few options were available for transportation because the school district did not provide a bus. A girl who lived in the general vicinity had a car and picked up a group of girls each day. She rather condescendingly offered a place in her backseat to Iris, who had no choice but to accept the ride. Iris was poorer than the other girls, and her clothes were not stylish. They made fun of her. Their teasing left deep scars that she carried with her for the rest of her life.

Iris and Avis in matching dresses, circa 1938

Their dresses were designed and then sewed by hand by their mother, Carrie.

Iris's experience was not unique. There are many accounts of rural kids during the late nineteenth and early twentieth centuries feeling put down by "townies." Laura Ingalls' nemesis, Nellie Oleson, felt superior to the poorer Laura, who lived in the country. And Rose, Laura's daughter, wrote in her journals her feelings about being poor and not fitting in with the girls in town. Joe, the hero of the *Betsy-Tacy* books by Maud Hart Lovelace, could not participate in any of the crowd's activities because he was poor and lived in the country.

Iris was well-versed on the American dream. She knew education was her way of achieving it. She had read every Horatio Alger book that she could find. Alger was a prolific author during the previous century. His books always had the same theme: a *rags to riches* narrative of an impoverished boy from a humble background who achieved middle-class security through hard work, determination, courage, and honesty. The stories always threw in a little luck, because there was usually some benefactor who rewarded the boy. These books inspired Iris. Although deeply hurt by the teasing, she persevered.

The next year, the school district provided a bus to transport the rural kids to school, but it was not free. It cost each family $1.50 per month. It sounds trivial today, but during the Great Depression, it was a significant amount. Somehow, their father, Finn, found the money so Iris and Avis could ride the bus. Every day, the bus passed a boy walking to school because his family chose not to pay the $1.50. The bus driver honked the horn and the boy smiled, laughed, and waved at the kids on the bus. One of the kids said, "That's Frank Sweaney!"

Frank's high school graduation picture, 1938

By his senior year in 1938, the school district paid for Frank to ride the bus. He sat beside Iris. Frank loved to discuss the issues of the day, and Iris was a willing listener. They not only talked about their high school classes, but about politics and world affairs. The Sweaneys were avid fans of Roosevelt. Frank challenged Iris's beliefs, but she held her own in their discussions. He had a sparkle in his eyes when he offered a clever retort to her opinions. It was all good fun and more than a little flirtatious as they argued and teased each other. Their banter entertained the other students. One of the younger kids remarked, "If Iris McCluey and Frank Sweaney ever get married, their children will be second Galileos."

Frank and Iris did get their high school education, but their future together would have to wait. Life does not always follow a direct path. There are curves on the road and bumps along the way. There are detours that take us away from our intended destination. It was so for my parents.

I Hear the
Rolling Thunder

Nineteen

It was 1939. Iris McCluey turned twenty-one that summer. At her high school commencement, she heard that her life was in front of her. She had no idea what that life would bring.

Iris McCluey in 1939

Iris did not graduate from high school until 1939. Her parents did not start her in school until she was eight. They held her back so that she and Avis could walk to school together.

The year 1939 was when Hollywood produced great movies. Dorothy followed the yellow brick road for the first time. Americans accompanied Mr. Smith to Washington and cheered as he brought down a corrupt system of cronyism with his Senate filibuster. John Wayne became an A-list movie star with his portrayal of the Ringo Kid in *Stagecoach*. However, people formed the longest lines to hear Rhett Butler tell Scarlett, "Frankly, my dear, I don't give a damn." David O. Selznick, the guiding force behind the movie production of Margaret Mitchell's bestseller *Gone with The Wind* had to fight to bring those words to movie audiences. Clark Gable's famous words ran afoul of the moral arbiters of the time. *Damn* was on the list of forbidden words of the Motion Picture Association's Production Code. Selznick held firm, and the line is now recognized by the American Film Institute as the number one movie quotation of all time.

In that pre-TV era, movies always were preceded by newsreels. Americans were entertained by the rich and famous frolicking at Newport. These scenes helped them escape the realities of their daily lives, still enmeshed in the toils of the Great Depression. The movies were also a counterbalance to the hard news in the newsreels. By 1939, the world was becoming scary. Benito Mussolini, the Italian Fascist, had invaded Ethiopia a few years earlier. Newsreels covered the ineffective response of the League of Nations. Now, the actions of his ally, Adolph Hitler, the funny looking German Chancellor with the little mustache, were increasingly featured. His armies took control of one European country after another, with no military opposition. England and France had pacts with Poland and warned Hitler that they would act if Germany invaded their ally. Hitler called their bluff and marched into Poland under the pretense of Polish aggression, which had actually been staged by Germans. On September 1, England and France declared war on Germany.

Across the Atlantic Ocean, the prevailing American sentiment was one of isolation: *Let the Europeans fight their own war.* The aviator Charles Lindbergh, America's great popular hero, was actively promoting "America First." Midwesterners had close ties to Europe and many carried German blood in their veins. Although alarmed over the news accounts of Hitler's aggression, people were war weary. America had joined with England to defeat the Hun during the Great War, and memories of that horrible struggle were still fresh. They were not ready to fight another war. As Emperor Hirohito and his Prime Minister Tojo were flexing their muscles by invading Manchuria and China, it was easy for most Americans to close their eyes to the growing danger in the Pacific.

As the world fell apart, Iris's personal life was a little unfocused. She worked odd jobs, which gave her a little money but helped her to develop into the woman that she would become. At a florist shop in nearby Lamar, she created flower arrangements. When I was a child, we visited South Missouri and always drove through Lamar. The town cemetery bordered the highway. Mom always pointed out the grave of a popular young girl from a well-known family. She had died in a car accident her senior year in high school. Her death haunted Iris for the rest of her life. She told how there were so many flower arrangements ordered for the funeral that the shop could not fill them all. She worked late into the night tying bows, hoping to comfort the mourners.

In 1940, Avis graduated from high school and joined her sister in the workforce as a telephone operator. The two girls formed a tight group with other young people, and the friends would gather at the bowling alley in Lockwood. Soon a skating rink was built and became another popular hangout. On weekends, they often attended movies at Lockwood's Cozy Theater. Sometime that year, the sisters bought a camera. They took pictures of their group of friends and taped the photos into a photo album. I loved looking at this album when I was a girl. It had stiff black pages with photos affixed to it with tape, yellowed with age by the time I looked at them during my childhood.

As I turned the pages of the album, there were more and more young men in the pictures. Frank Sweaney was not one of them. He left Dade County as soon as he graduated from high school in 1938. With a small scholarship from Sears and Roebuck, and by working odd jobs along the way, he was able to pay for college. By the time these pictures were taken, he was studying chemistry and biology at the University of Missouri in Columbia. However, one young man's face appeared often. His name was Johnny. He was a brother of one of the girls in the group. His face matched the words that Avis wrote about him: *Johnny was lots of fun, but he was not good material for a husband.* It took Iris a little while to figure that out. Halfway through the album, Johnny shows up in an Army uniform.

The news from Europe had not been good. France had fallen to the Nazis on June 22, 1940, and England seemed to be on the verge of collapsing. Along with the rest of America, the McCluey girls listened to Edward R. Murrow on the radio. His broadcasts brought the horrors of the London Blitz into American homes. From September 7, 1940, until May of 1941, the Nazi Luftwaffe relentlessly bombed civilian London. "This is London," Murrow said at the beginning of his reports. In the background, Americans heard air raid sirens and bombs exploding.

President Franklin D. Roosevelt and his advisors worried that America was not ready to fight a war. Our army was understaffed and untrained. One historian said that in 1940, America's army was smaller than the army of Portugal. On September 16, 1940, FDR signed a bill authorizing America's first peacetime draft. All American males between twenty-one and thirty-six had to register. The government selected those to serve through a lottery system. Before the end of the year, men were reporting for duty. The promise was that they would only have to serve a year and then they would be sent home—and their service would be stateside or in an American territory.

Johnny was an early draftee. Iris accompanied him to the station in Lockwood to catch a train to his base in Texas. It was a tearful goodbye, and Iris and Johnny made promises to each other. The same scene was played out in train stations across the country. On the radio, the Prairie Ramblers crooned a popular song of the day, "I'll Be Back In A Year (Little Darlin')":

> I'll be back in a year little darlin'
> Uncle Sam has called and I must go
> I'll be back don't you fear little darlin'
> You'll be proud of your soldier boy I know
>
> I'll do my best each day for the good ol' USA
> And we'll keep Old Glory waving high
> I'll be back in a year little darlin'
> Don't you worry darlin' don't you cry

Buoyed by the success of this song, the group quickly produced an answer song, "I'll Be Waiting for You," with the vocal sung by female artist Gale Ryan:

> I'll be waiting for you, darling
> While you do your bit for Uncle Sam
> I'll be brave and true my darling
> And help the U.S.A. the best I can
>
> I'm proud to see you go and proud I'll be, I know
> For you will keep Old Glory high above
> I'll be waiting for you, darling
> True to the soldier boy I love

By the summer of 1941, Roosevelt knew that he could not let the draftees go home. The situation in Europe was clearly deteriorating, and many believed that it was just a matter of time before America would be at war. Murrow's broadcasts had moved the needle of public sentiment in America from isolation toward engagement on the side of England. On August 12, the United States House of Representatives approved the extension of the peacetime draft by a single vote. The Senate approved it by a wider margin, and Roosevelt signed the bill into law on August 18.

Some of the early draftees threatened to desert once their original twelve months were up. They felt justified in doing so since the government had changed the terms of their agreement. They painted the letters O H I O on the walls of their barracks in protest. These letters were an acronym for Over the Hill in October, indicating that they would desert upon the end of their twelve months of duty, although very few followed through with the threat.

Then, on a Sunday morning in December, the question became moot. The Japanese bombed Pearl Harbor. We were at war.

Congress passed a new Selective Service Act that stated men between eighteen and forty-five were liable for military service and all men between eighteen and sixty-five were required to register. The term of service was extended to six months after the war.

Radios stopped playing "I'll Be Back In A Year (Little Darlin')."

Twenty

Lockwood sent its young men to war. Soon, houses in town had a blue star in the window, signifying that a family member was serving in the military.

President Roosevelt recruited everyone to the struggle: "There is one front and one battle where everyone in the United States—every man, woman, and child—is in action, and will be privileged to remain in action throughout this war. That front is right here at home, in our daily lives, and in our daily tasks." Lockwood listened and acted. The Immanuel Lutheran Church resolved to donate ten percent of its Sunday collections for the purchase of government Defense Bonds. Churches invited men stationed at nearby Camp Crowder to their services, and its military band played at outdoor concerts in the town. The city council bought a new American flag to fly over the city building. Local citizens organized a Junk Rally proclaiming that "Junk helps make guns, tanks, and ships for our fighting men … throw YOUR scrap into the fight."

The war effort was all-important. All had to sacrifice. The needs of the fighting men came first. By the spring of 1942, the government's Office of Price Administration issued ration books containing stamps to all American families. Rationing was intended to ensure fairness, since all Americans, regardless of wealth, theoretically had equal access to the limited commodities. The first books were called Sugar Books, since Japanese action in the Pacific had cut off the sugar imports. Before long coffee, meat, cheese, butter, and other commodities were rationed. Finn and other farmers were still able to get gas to power tractors, but fuel for nonessential travel was controlled. Iris and Avis had to do without stockings since both silk and nylon were needed for parachutes. Some girls in their crowd used leg makeup, and with a marker drew a black line on the back of their legs to simulate a stocking seam.

Lockwood marked the first anniversary of the war with a blackout. Ninety-eight percent of the community participated. Lockwood citizens wanted to be prepared in case they would need to turn off lights to protect their community from enemy night bombing raids, despite the fact that this tiny community in rural Missouri was probably not a high priority strategic bombing target. Community leaders were designated as air raid wardens. The drill began when Avis, at the local telephone switchboard, rang each home one time. People turned out all lights almost instantly, and the first responders acted out their parts. In spite of the seriousness of war, the town folks enjoyed the simulation.

There was an unintended benefit to the war. It brought jobs to Lockwood and the other towns in Southwest Missouri. A defense plant opened in town to make crates for trailer tanks. The crates held water tanks that supplied water to the men on the front. The workers felt that they were contributing to the war effort; after all, it was just as vital that our boys have water as ammunition. Nearby in Neosho, civilians found jobs at Camp Crowder, the army's training center for the Signal Corps. Heavily guarded troop trains rolled through the town, some going south, some north, carrying guns, tanks, jeeps, and men.

At night, Iris wrote to Johnny. All her girlfriends were writing to a serviceman. Even if they were not truly in love, it was their patriotic duty. The *Lockwood Luminary*, published the military APO addresses of local men. Iris had no trouble following the words of Gale Ryan's song. "Being True" was relatively easy. There were few young men left in Lockwood. However, for her *soldier boy*, it was a different story. One day she received a letter from Johnny, still stationed stateside in Texas. He told her that he had met another girl. His new girlfriend was going to have a baby and he felt he should marry her. Iris wrote back and said, "Yes, I think you should marry her." Her sister Avis later wrote that it was "*a blessing*" that they broke up.

I never thought that Johnny really broke my mother's heart, but she probably felt that she was at a crossroads. The door to a life that she had imagined was now closed. Regardless, she picked up the pieces of her damaged ego and moved on. That summer she and Avis attended summer school at Southwest Baptist College in Bolivar, Missouri. The money made from their odd jobs allowed them to pay the tuition, room, and board. There was not much money left over, and the girls could not afford to buy a suitcase, so they packed their few dresses and other items in a cardboard box.

Iris loved that summer. She was challenged and did well in her classes. She was inspired by Professor Beasley's history class and enjoyed writing the required papers. Her yearbooks from her summers at Southwest Baptist College are full of signatures and warm notes from the girls that she met. She looks very young, pretty, and happy in the yearbook photos. The men in her college classes were not appealing to her. She felt that many of them were attempting to avoid the draft by becoming ministers. With the men all gone to war and

Avis and Iris at College

*Avis and Iris are in the center of the group of women
in their college yearbook photo.*

jobs plentiful in the defense industry, there was a shortage of
teachers. That summer, Iris took the required state teacher
examinations. Even without a college degree, she was offered
a teaching position in a rural one-room school. She signed
a contract with Dade County on September 2, 1942, and
agreed to teach for a term of eight months for a sum of $45 a
month. The contract indicated that this compensation covered
janitorial duties. She would be paid monthly if she performed
her duties and her reports were correctly made.

Twenty-One

Iris was assigned to teach the Stone School that she and Avis had attended as children. It was out in the country, not far from McCluey land.

It was one of several one-room rural schools in Dade County. Missouri had such schools until the middle of the 1960s. A few students in my high school graduating class in 1970 started first grade in a schoolhouse that combined grades together. My romantic image of one-room schools was first formed by the *Little House* books. Laura Ingalls taught in such a school before she married Almanzo Wilder, and her challenges of teaching her students filled chapters of *These Happy Golden Years*. I fantasized about going to such a school and was jealous of the kids in my class that had started their school days in such a setting. I pictured my mother as the heroine of my favorite books. I imagined that her experiences had been just like Laura's.

But my mother's world was different than Laura's. America had changed in the five decades since Laura had taught at the Brewster School. In Laura's time, there were only thirty-eight states, and the Dakota land was just a territory. In 1942, forty-eight stars adorned the flag, one for each state in the Union. America truly stretched from "sea to shining sea." Iris's students began the morning by reciting the Pledge of

Allegiance to this flag. Laura could not have begun her day in such a manner since the pledge was not written until 1892. With patriotic sentiment at a high point, Congress formally adopted these words as our pledge in 1942, and Americans said their allegiance with great zeal.

It was recited with almost religious fervor, although "under God" was not added to the creed until the following decade, in 1954. However, there was a problem. Men, women, and children delivered the words by extending their right arm straight forward, fingers outstretched. Hitler had usurped that salute and Americans were horrified to think that they looked like Nazis saying "Heil Hitler" when saluting Old Glory. On December 22, 1942, Congress passed a resolution. It called for Americans to place their right hands over their hearts, showing their heartfelt loyalty to their country when saying the pledge. So the students at the Stone School started each day by pledging their loyalty to their flag and country with their hands over their hearts.

A globe sat in the corner of the Stone classroom. The land masses and oceans looked the same as those on the globe in Laura's classroom, but the lines defining the borders of the countries had changed. After World War I, new borders were created in Europe, reallocating land that had once been under German control. The Third Reich reclaimed these lands, and the German army marched across the lines on the globe. The German swastika now hung in France, Austria, Czechoslovakia, and Poland. In the Pacific, Japan was increasingly ignoring the sovereign rights of its neighbors.

For the students at the Stone School, their globe was a reminder that events in faraway places affected their lives. Their fathers, older brothers, and neighbors had left home and were wearing uniforms. Most men were still stateside, but each child knew that could soon change. By the fall of 1942, the Japanese had killed Americans on islands in the Pacific Ocean. General MacArthur was forced to leave the Philippines. Although he promised "I shall return," this did not seem to be imminent. America's naval victory at Midway Island in the Pacific was encouraging, and Iris had her students locate that island on their globe.

Iris was charged with keeping her students' attention on their studies. Like all good teachers, she knew the importance of a structured day. After the pledge was said, her students recited the Lord's Prayer. Before she started the lessons, Iris read a chapter from a novel to the class. Like her mother, Carrie, who had read out loud to her family, Iris had an expressive reading voice. The class listened to various books, and one of their favorites was Gene Stratton Porter's novel *Girl of the Limberlost*. Porter was an avid naturalist and early ecologist. The story appealed to the rural kids of Southwest Missouri who recognized her depiction of the outdoors. The book's emphasis on the importance of education was a message Iris valued.

The Stone pupils called their teacher Miss Iris. She especially loved the little ones and later wrote:

> *I worried about starting children out, but I have found it pretty easy so far. I wish you could have seen one of my first graders last year. At the end of school, he could read better than anyone I had in school, knew letter sounds, could add and subtract, and knew a lot of his multiplication tables.*

It was one of the benefits of a school that had different grades in one room. The smart little ones learned the lessons given to the older children. Math was taught in the traditional manner, with a heavy emphasis on memorization of the classic algorithms. The students wrote their arithmetic problems on the board with chalk. Science classes were practical, with experiments that conveyed basic scientific facts.

They learned America's story. They read Longfellow's version of Paul Revere's ride and memorized the Preamble to the U.S. Constitution and Lincoln's Gettysburg's Address. They studied the presidents of the United States whose pictures were in the classroom. But there was only one president who was relevant to the students, for they had only known one: Franklin Delano Roosevelt. He had been president for over a decade. In the fall of 1940, he broke with the tradition established by George Washington that presidents should have only two terms. He ran for a third term and won.

Penmanship was valued. There was a poster of the alphabet in the classroom that showed the correct formation of both capital and lower case letters. Iris modeled the cursive script by writing wise sayings on the blackboard, and then her students discussed their meaning. Students, even the youngest, studied and memorized poetry:

> This old world we live in
> Is mighty hard to beat,
> You get a thorn with every rose,
> But aren't the roses sweet.

And in March, as the wind blew in from the west, the students recited:

> The March wind blows the washing
> And twists it on the line

It pushes me along the street
And steals Jane's hat and mine
But, I don't mind the weather,
It makes me want to sing
For, I know its pushing winter out
And making room for spring.

Iris came in early each day to sweep the floor. Her students often volunteered at the end of the day to help her clean the chalkboards. They took erasers and hit them together to clear out the chalk dust. As spring came to Missouri, it was a blessing that she no longer had to bring coal into the small building to heat it. She had been worried that with the wartime shortages, she might deplete her coal supply before the spring thaw.

As the school year came to a close, Iris made plans to return to summer school at Bolivar. Her sister Avis was also teaching, although not in Dade County; she was in Northern Missouri, staying with her mother's sister Elba, and teaching in a small one-room school there. Iris and Avis missed each other but wrote frequently. As soon as her school year ended, Avis came back to Dade County. The girls packed their clothes again in boxes and used their teaching proceeds to pay the $85 for tuition and room and board required for the summer session at Southwest Baptist College.

This time, as she sat in her college classes, she knew that in September she would return to the Stone School. She had already signed a contract to teach again for the school year 1943-1944.

Twenty-Two

By the fall of 1943, Missouri's young men (some little more than boys) were stationed all over the world. Units from Dade County were in England. Clearly there were plans in the works to invade France. Every person in Lockwood knew someone who was overseas. People lived with a sense of anxiety. The war news was not always good. Progress was being made in Italy, but it came with heavy casualties.

In April, 1944, Pfc. Vencil Woody of Carthage, Missouri, sent a poem home to his parents. He wrote, *I want the people at home to read this, and then they may know some of the things we are going through here in Italy.* The *Luminary* published it.

WE DID OUR STRETCH IN HELL

I am sitting here and thinking
of the things I left behind
and I hate to put in writing
what is running through my mind.

But there's one good consolation,
so gather around me while I tell,
we will all go to heaven
for we did our stretch in hell.

We have stood a million guard mounts,

we have cleaned up our latrines.
We have waded through the marshes
of a million tons of mud.
We have killed a million insects
that tried to suck our blood.

When the final taps have sounded
and we lay aside life's cares;
when we stand that last inspection
on those shining golden stairs,
the angels then will welcome us,
their magic harps will play;
we'll draw a million canteen checks
and spend them in a day.

It is there we will hear St. Peter
tell us loudly with a yell,
"Take a seat, deserving soldiers,
for you've done your stretch in hell."

Easter that year fell on April 9. Iris decided to buy a card in honor of the holiday to send to an old high school friend; she had seen his address in the *Luminary*. It took a little while for a reply to come.

It was postmarked May 29, 1944, and was mailed from someplace in the Aleutian Islands. These islands were part of America's Alaska territory. Military operations in the Aleutians started early in the war, in June of 1942. A small Japanese force invaded the islands in an attempt to control Pacific transportation routes. The islands were the only U.S. territory occupied by the Japanese during World War II. Consequently, the Aleutians were not only of strategic value to the war effort, but their occupation was a blow to American morale. Although the Japanese force was small, weather conditions and harsh terrain worked in Japan's favor, and it took more than a year for the Americans to completely expel the enemy.

On the outside of the envelope was a stamp indicating that it had been opened and read by military censors. It was a letter that changed Iris' life.

The first page of Frank Sweaney's handwritten letter to Iris McCluey

890th Chemical Co.
(Air Operations)
1st Platoon A.P.O. 980
c/o Postmaster
Seattle, Washington

Dear Iris,

Somewhere in the "Aleutian area," a few days ago I received your nice card and want to take the privilege of thanking you for the remembrance. I received the Luminary here and see in it that you are becoming quite a success as a school teacher. The last time I saw you was when you, Billy and Avis come by our place about two years ago. at that time you were not teaching but working for Mrs. Bowels in Lockwood

This letter changed Iris's life.

890th Chemical Company
(Air Operations)
1st Platoon A.P.O 980
C/o Postmaster
Seattle, Washington

Dear Iris,

Somewhere in the "Aleutian Area," a few days ago I received your nice card and want to take the privilege of thanking you for the remembrance. I receive the Luminary here and see in it that you are becoming quite a success as a school teacher. The last time I saw you was when you, Billy, and Avis came by our place about two years ago. At that time you were not teaching and working for Mrs. Bowels in Lockwood. I intended to look you up as I went back to Columbia but never had the chance. I saw Avis in Lockwood about a year ago today at the skating rink. Since that time, I've been mostly overseas.

My brother and I have been in the army now almost 2 years. Since that time I've traveled from home to the east coast from the east coast to the gulf and from there to the Canadian border, from there to the west coast and finally overseas. Alaska isn't much different from Missouri except that it is considerably cooler. The "Aleutian area" is far different, being mostly fog, rain, snow and wind.

I see by your address that you are at Bolivar and assume that you are attending Southwest Baptist, a nice place if I remember correctly.

No place can be much nicer than Missouri was to me. However, it is pretty much the results of being there that

I wound up here in a chemical company. Graduated in 42 with a chemistry-biology major and had gone back to spend about 6 months working on a masters when I was drafted, so with what chemistry I had they decided chemical warfare was where I belonged, so here I am in a very safe, dull, monotonous place in a chemical air operations unit.

I'd really be glad to see the states again and best of all Southwest Missouri.

Thanks again for the card. Would enjoy hearing from you if you care to write. I should have written you after you came by that day, but sorry to say just didn't do it. Best wishes for more success in that teaching field.

An old friend,
Frank Sweaney

Frank Sweaney and his buddies, WWII

This picture was taken somewhere in the Aleutian Area. Frank is the last man on the right-hand side of the photo.

A few days after Iris received this letter, the citizens of Lockwood, Missouri, went to church. It was the middle of the week, Tuesday, June 6, 1944, *Invasion Day*. The people did not yet call it D-Day. It was seven in the morning when word was received in Southwest Missouri that American, British, and Canadian troops had landed in France. Local sirens sounded. As the *Luminary* noted, many felt the need for a haven for *"prayer and solace for hearts that were heavy."* Almost immediately, people went to the Methodist and Baptist churches. All places of business closed from nine to ten o'clock to give people the time to pray.

There were people in the community whose petitions to God were personal. Their sons or husbands had been in England, some as long as two years, preparing for the invasion. They did not yet know if the men they loved had survived the bloody assault on the Normandy Beaches.

Twenty-Three

Frank left the Aleutians in June of 1944. For a few months, the army moved him around the country. He joked in a letter, *If that old saying about a rolling stone gathering no moss applies in my case, I should be getting quite 'a sheen.'* The army did grant him a furlough and he went back home. He did not immediately contact Iris. He had not yet received any encouragement from her. The army mail system was unable to keep up with his movements, and her reply to his letter was lost in limbo.

One day during that furlough, Frank was sitting at a café in Lockwood in his army uniform, drinking a cup of coffee with a sailor also home on leave. He just happened to see Iris across the street. It was the first time in weeks she had gone to town. Frank got up from his table and ran across the street to her. They spent the day together, and they both believed that it was fate that they saw each other again.

Six years had passed since they last spoke. Those years changed them, took them in different directions, and both grew up a little. College expanded their worlds and gave them new horizons to explore. Now in their mid-twenties, their lives intersected again and they came to each other as adults. They went home that night knowing something important had happened. And for the next year and half, Iris McCluey and Frank Sweaney lived for their mail.

In their letters, they shared the love they each felt for their families. Although they had attended the same small high school, their families did not know each other. The Sweaneys differed from the hard-working Calvinistic McCluey dirt farmers. The Sweaneys were Ozark people who loved telling stories, laughing, and fishing. Their close-knit family was all important to them. Frank's mother, Eva Alice Sweaney, was the soul of the family. She married at fourteen and delivered Frank, her first son, the next year. Woodrow came along soon afterwards. Then there was a surprise. About the time Frank was leaving home, Evie Sweaney had another baby, a little girl named Goldie. Frank doted on his baby sister, and his letters to Iris were full of stories about her.

Frank's family did not really understand him. He always had his nose in a book. It was a big deal for him to leave home and go to college almost two hundred miles away. His fun-loving younger brother, Woodie, had followed the more traditional path of Sweaney men. He loved the outdoors and was bored with school. Woodie enjoyed a good story and could spin a tale with the best of them. But in 1942, Uncle Sam made no distinction between the two brothers. The Dade County Draft Board called both Sweaney boys to serve. They joined the army together. Their mother wanted it that way. She expected them to take care of each other. Although the official military regulations discouraged brothers from serving in the same unit, the Sweaney boys were like many other siblings who wanted to be together, and so the regulation was overlooked. Frank and Woodrow's first army pictures show them laughing, with the much larger Woodrow's arm slung around his older brother's shoulder.

On November 13, 1942, the Japanese sank the American light cruiser *Juneau* during the Battle of Guadalcanal. On it were the five Sullivan brothers from Waterloo, Iowa. They all perished. The Fighting Sullivans became the American symbol of family sacrifice, and their parents made appearances around the country selling war bonds. Recruiting posters showed the five brothers with the caption "They Did Their Part." A destroyer was named in their honor. Most importantly for Frank and Woodrow Sweaney, the armed forces decided to strictly enforce the policy that siblings could not serve together. The two brothers were separated. Their mother never forgave the army for going back on the promise that her two boys would be together. It was part of the Sweaney code that the family watched out for each other. From the Aleutians, Woodrow was sent to Fort Benning, Georgia, and Frank was sent on various training assignments around the country. Rumors were that Frank's outfit would soon be sent overseas.

Iris wrote Frank of her family. She shared the adventures of Avis, who was teaching in Northern Missouri. Her sister was writing letters to her own serviceman. Richard was an older brother of two cute little boys that she was teaching in her one-room school. Iris also wrote Frank of her concerns for her older sister, Gwen. Gwen's life was not easy. Like Woodie, she did not finish high school. Due to bad luck and unfortunate decisions, she was raising two small children and needed both emotional and financial support. Her two sisters loved Gwen's children and tried to help the young struggling family as best they could.

Frank's letters contained vivid descriptions of a United States that Iris had never seen. He was temporarily stationed at Fort Meade, near D.C., "a very nice camp," in his opinion. He regrettably knew that he would not be there long. Fort Meade was serving only as a replacement center. While there, he wrote her of busy wartime Washington. With a weekend pass, he toured the sights of the Capital. He described the statues of Lincoln and Will Rogers but especially enjoyed the treasures that he saw at the Smithsonian.

From D.C., his company was sent to Fort Shelby, Mississippi. The United States he saw there concerned him. He wrote Iris of an America that was fighting discrimination abroad but that had not yet come to grips with its own history and demons. The country boy from the Ozark Mountains was appalled and wrote her:

> *An incident happened on the way down here that shows, to me at least, very vividly how the racial problem is still going strong in the south* [sic]. *There was a negro* [sic] *solider on the train who had been wounded in Sicily and was returning home for a rest. He went into the station at Memphis to get something to eat. He first went to the negro* [sic] *café—yes here colored can't eat in the same place as the whites—there he was told they didn't serve whites. He wasn't dark enough to be called a negro* [sic] *by them. He then went to the white restaurant where he didn't get anything to eat because they said he was a negro* [sic]. *He tried different places until train time and finally had to board the train without anything to eat for at least 16 hrs I know. It struck me as rather queer that he was good enough to fight for his country and good enough to be wounded, yet the people here didn't think he was good enough to eat in the same place they did. So you see 1865 still lives in the South. I wouldn't have believed anything like that could happen until I actually saw that occur.*

Iris responded with her own feelings about discrimination:

I never will believe it is right to discriminate between white and black people. God made us both and I believe he intended the Negro to have equal privileges with the white man. I believe if we helped the Negro and gave him a chance at an education he would do some very constructive work.

The army prepared troops for combat at Fort Shelby. Frank's training became focused:

Got assigned today and from the looks of things I'm going to be in a pretty interesting company. Am in what they call the Pioneer platoon which is the ones who handle the ammunitions, explosives etc. Don't know many more of the details yet, but next to the war being over I couldn't ask for anything else.

Frank knew full well that dealing with explosives could be dangerous even in a noncombat role. There was an incident in the Aleutians that still haunted him:

The worst scare I've had since I've been in the army was in that work. Up in the Aleutians myself and another man were moving blasting caps and bomb fuses. Your dad knows how sensitive they are to shock. Anyway we were unloading them off a truck and carrying them into the house which was holding about 50,000 of the caps. The fuses were in 140+ boxes. This fellow walked in the building and in the place of putting the box down carefully just opened his hands and rather nonchalantly let it fall to the floor from about waist high. A miracle must have happened because any other time they would have been picking us and the truck up with tweezers, but it didn't go off. The other men said for weeks afterwards that that was the first time they ever saw me really mad. We were both corporals at the time and he happened to be in charge, but that didn't make much difference. I'm afraid that I really got him told off and told quickly, then I walked off and left the job with him. A man may know everything possible about those explosives, but he never knows enough, and any time he can get that careless he is forgetting what he's doing, he should get some other job. That fellow immediately hollered that he knew they wouldn't go off. But never can one man's ideas to carelessness be accepted in a case like that as an excuse. I'll never forget that moment as long as I live. I can claim it is one time I was really mad and disgusted in this army. All that training had been wasted on that man as far as I was concerned.

Now in Mississippi, Frank was given more training in explosives. He was thrown into an intensive program in munitions and had daily grenade practice:

We've been awfully busy here at Camp Shelby. The last few days we're studying explosives and setting them off blowing down trees and such. Really interesting, but at times rather nerve-wracking.

Clearly, these men were being prepared for deployment. No one believed that they would be in Mississippi for long. Frank watched as new friends in other units were sent to join the fighting that was raging across Europe and on islands in the Pacific. He exchanged addresses with several of these men. They would correspond frequently during the next year. Then the word came down to his unit. The rumors had been right. As Frank wrote, *This war will not be won at home.* His outfit was leaving the continental U.S. They were headed to Panama.

Twenty-Four

Frank's unit would not cross the Rhine, fight in the Battle of the Bulge, or raise the flag on Iwo Jima. However, none of the men in Company G of the 150th Infantry Regiment doubted that protecting the canal from sabotage by the Axis powers was of vital importance. The canal was the link between the Atlantic and Pacific Oceans. American and allied ships passed through it on the way to the Pacific. Without the canal, ships built and staffed in shipyards along America's East Coast would have had to go almost an additional eight thousand miles around the tip of South America in order to bring men and needed supplies to the war raging in the Pacific. The tide of the war might change if ships could not pass through the canal. Consequently, its defense was the major U.S. concern in the American Theater.

On November 11, 1944, Frank wrote his first letter to Iris from this hot, wet, tropical land. He was to be there for the next year. She opened each letter carefully, preserving the envelope, with its censorship stamp. She was not the first person to have read the letter. It had been opened and reviewed by a military censor whose job was to ensure that Frank had not accidently written anything that could be used by the enemy if somehow it fell into their hands. Iris read each letter several times before putting it back in its envelope and placing it with the others in her special keepsake box.

He could not share many of his observations about Panama, specifics about his activities, or even his location with her until military censorship was lifted in September of 1945. Three years earlier, he never could have pictured himself sitting in a guard tower high above the Panama Canal. That Sunday morning in December of 1941 seemed so long ago. The "day that will live in infamy" had changed his life. Frank Sweaney, a boy from the Ozark Mountains of Missouri, was now in a land that he had only read about in books and performing what he considered to be a very important job. After the war was over, he wrote to Iris:

> *Sugar, to start with I'll tell you where we are located. It is at Miraflores Locks in the Panama Canal. It is the last lock before reaching to the Pacific Ocean and is located on the South side of the Isthmus of Panama. We've been here since we once got assigned in Panama. All we do is pull guard. We are on guard sometime each day. One week we are on guard from six in the morning until noon. This week we are on from midnight until six in the morning. We then have off 18 hours out of twenty-four during which we are supposed to get our rest and do whatever details we might have to do. Six hours doesn't sound like much, but down here that is an awful lot of work a day, for the humidity is so high that it really makes a person tired.*

> *The army took over the canal in 1941 and before that all civilians did the guarding. I imagine now that it will be returned back to them, how soon is hard to say. We really had a big job here. It is a very vulnerable position and has had to really have a heavy guard. Working here are men from*

practically all the walks of life and every country as that a very careful check has to be maintained at all time ... It is just lucky that the Japs hit Pearl Harbor instead of here for if they had hit here instead and been as lucky, I'm sure the we wouldn't have celebrated VJ day this year...One good saboteur that had slipped in could have wrecked things for a long while.

You see boats from every nation in the world going through here. Besides being always on the alert against sabotage we've got to do our best to maintain a good impression on the other countries. We have had to work hard, but when it is all said and done we have been pretty lucky and you don't hear too much "petty griping." We all feel we have done a pretty fair job here and let it go at that.

However, Frank was bored and more than a little homesick. The Japanese assault on the canal did not happen. Other than mandatory guard duty, he had little to do. He filled his time by visiting the camp library, going to movies, reading any book that caught his attention, and writing letters. Letters were his connection to the world beyond his hot barracks. He wrote to his mother, his buddies overseas, and friends from college. Most of all, he wrote to "his girl, Iris." He waited impatiently each day for mail call.

Iris wrote nice, newsy letters full of stories about her everyday life on the home front:

Did you know it is almost impossible to buy soap here in the states now? I used the last of my laundry soap Friday. Guess I'll be washing my clothes without soap.

She shared with him her college experiences; he loved hearing about them. He had thrived during his years at the University of Missouri. Her letters brought back those happy times. He gave her advice on her challenging arithmetic class. She shared stories about her favorite teacher, Professor Beasley, and the ideas she heard in his history class. In turn, Frank wrote about the songs on the radio, the men in his unit, and movies he saw, including *Meet Me in St. Louis*, which he recommended to Iris. He wrote about the books he was reading and articles that he found in magazines. Iris looked up the articles in her college library, and by reading them, she felt closer to him.

Iris in 1944

Frank taped a picture of "his girl" to his bunk and looked at her face while he wrote his letters.

When her summer school was over and she was in charge of her own one-room classroom, she entertained him with stories about her young students. She had a few ornery boys and there was always some anecdote about their behavior to pass on to him. She shared with him her plans for a neighborhood pie supper. Her students were practicing their recitations to show their parents how much they were learning. It was a world that he knew well, and her stories took him back home.

She also sent him news of the boys from Dade County far from home. There was a local boy killed on Omaha Beach and others lost as G.I.s marched across France. Their parents had received the dreaded telegram. The blue star in their window was now a gold star. She told him of their friend from high school who had been shot down over France and was now in a German POW camp. She shared stories of her girlfriends and the men they loved who were off fighting.

He wrote her of the letters he received from his buddies now in Europe and the Pacific:

> *I received a letter today from a boy named Verne Murray who lives there close to home and he is now on Okinawa. He says he has been in the invasion of Leyte and in the Okinawa operations and has yet to fire a shot. He writes that that doesn't mean he hasn't been fired at. He said that the night before he wrote me that the "Japs" had laid down an artillery barrage on them and that he had spent most of the night in the foxhole. He said between praying and digging he didn't know which he did most of. He claims that it really made a Christian out of him. He is a man who isn't very easily scared either. Those fellows in the combat zone really do have it rough.*

And they both wrote of their sorrow of learning on April 12, 1945, that President Roosevelt had died. Unlike most Americans who had never really heard of Harry S Truman, Iris and Frank knew about him; after all, he had been born in nearby Lamar, in Barton County, and had been their senator. President Truman was one of them, a Missourian.

In less than a month after FDR died, Germany fell and peace was declared in Europe. Even though Japan brought America into the War with its surprise attack on Pearl Harbor, FDR and Churchill devised a "Germany First" strategy. Although they were not openly presented to the American people, military plans emphasized the European theater first. The goal was to end Hitler's threat to the world and then shift all American resources to the Pacific.

Victory in Europe (V–E) Day on May 8 was a nice birthday present for President Truman. Frank wrote Iris that night:

V-E day here in Panama hasn't been much different than any other day. Those men who were on duty continued that way. It so happened that today was our group's day off. It seemed as if it were gradually building up to our day off before it could become official. Most of us gave a general thanks that it was over in Europe and that was our form of celebration. A few will probably come in tonight slightly polluted but as a rule I think this will be about as temperate a celebration as the end of any war has ever been.

It is good to know that those things represented by Nazi Germany will be no more, but then the problem of Japan just becomes more prominent. I think most of us here never thought of Japan as much of an enemy even after the tremendous progress they made in the early part of the war. Now we are rapidly finding ourselves thinking about them and when you are talking to a fellow tonight you'll find him starting his conversation with "I wonder ...." And then it is about Japan. It was very sad that President Roosevelt could not have lived to give the victory day speech after he had worked so hard for the end of the mess over there in Europe. President Truman's message was our first official word here. Many listened to the Prime Minister's speech instead. Then throughout the day those of us who have been fortunate to be near a radio have heard everyone from General Marshall to the man on the street give his ideas. All in all it has been a pretty swell day and darling I can frankly say that tonight my morale has rapidly soared upward. The only thing that will help it any more is some mail tomorrow. There was none today as the post office was closed. I get just somewhat blue when no mail comes, and usually it is uncalled for. There is always some logical explanation when there is none.

Frank's thoughts took on a personal note. The day they would see each other again might be just around the corner. With all the might of America aimed at the Pacific, surely the "Japs" would soon be defeated.

The main thing I liked about the end of the European mess was that at least a person has reached the place where his plans for the future may be put into practice one of these times. At any rate, we may be sort of safe in assuming that we are better than half-way [sic] done in our job, don't you think so?

I am not able to write of anything tonight except the war it seems. You probably will be pretty bored with reading about what I think. I had reached such a stage of expectancy that when the official announcement actually did come the edge had worn off quite a bit.

Frank's picture of Europe came not only from the official army reports, but also from his buddies there:

I got a letter from a boy I was with in Camp Shelby, Mississippi last summer. He is with Patton's third army, and writes about the beautiful places he is seeing. He is living now in some old remodeled castle and says he has at last a chance to really see how beautiful the country there is. Since the war ended he has probably just began [sic] to realize how sweet life is and [how] everything looks nice.

It must really be an odd feeling one day to have been doing your best to kill a group of men and the next day doing your best to rebuild their homes and lives. That's what is happening there now.

Frank and Iris were now optimistic. They were not alone in this feeling. Couples separated by continents began to plan for that day when there would be no more fighting and American men would be home safe and sound. The morale was upbeat, and the Armed Forces Radio repeatedly played Doris Day's hit song, "My Dreams Are Getting Better All the Time":

Well, what do you know, he smiled at me in my
    dreams last night
My dreams are getting better all the time
And, what do you know, he smiled at me in a different
    light
My dreams are getting better all the time
To think that we were strangers a couple of nights ago
And though it's a dream, I never dreamed he'd ever
    say hello
Oh, maybe tonight I'll hold him tight when the
    moonbeams shine

My dreams are getting better all the time

The song took on a special meaning for the young couple. They both allowed themselves to dream of the time when the war would end. Sometime during those months, perhaps even without being conscious of it, their dreams merged.

In Missouri, Iris heard the song and was lost in romantic thoughts. Frank listened to the song in Panama and dreamed of his life after the war. Sitting up high, guarding the Panama Canal, Frank planned his life. He knew he was going to go back to school, but instead of becoming a chemist, he was going to medical school. He knew he was to be a doctor. He wanted Iris by his side.

As the Brass in Washington made life and death decisions regarding which troops would be part of the invasion of Japan, Frank Sweaney and his buddies waited to learn their fate. And while he waited, Frank wrote Iris, often three times a day. No longer were their letters just between two high school friends. Even though Frank knew that military censors were reading every word, his daily letters were full of his growing love for her. McClueys did not openly share their feelings, and no one had ever made Iris feel this special.

The letters that she now received from Frank no longer started with *Dear Iris* as a greeting. When she opened the flimsy airmail paper, she saw the words *My dearest darling*. And instead of the signature *An old friend, Frank*, she read, *I will love you forever, Frank*.

Twenty-Five

Iris heard shouting in the halls of her dormitory at Southwest Baptist College. It was Tuesday, August 14, 1945. She quickly got caught up in the excitement of those around her. Japan had agreed to an unconditional surrender. So much had happened in the last few weeks. Just eight days earlier, the world had changed.

The United States dropped the atomic bomb on the Japanese city of Hiroshima on August 6. It was followed by a second atomic bomb on Nagasaki three days later. It was impossible for Frank and Iris to comprehend the full significance of the atomic bomb or predict its effect on future generations. They both tried to put their heads around this new weapon in their letters to each other. Frank went to the library and read anything unclassified he could find about atomic energy and this powerful new weapon. He wrote Iris about the research on atomic energy conducted by other countries, including the Axis powers. Iris always found God's providential hand in events, and responded:

> I think the atomic bomb is the greatest evidence that we have that God was on our side. The other nations had done so much work on it and yet He gave us that great discovery.

Neither one questioned that it was right for the United States to drop the bomb. They believed without any doubt in the righteousness of the cause. President Truman had to do anything in his power to bring the war to a close and minimize the loss of American lives.

For the last week, Iris and Frank had been on pins and needles. Surely the war would end soon. Each scribbled a note to the other person when a new development came over the radio. Between the two atomic blasts, the Soviet Union officially declared war on Japan on August 8 and poured more than a million Russian troops into Japanese-occupied Manchuria. Iris responded when she heard this news:

> *When something good happens my first impulse is to write to you. This afternoon, when I heard Russia had declared war on Japan, I wanted to write to you right then. Honey, it surely won't be so much longer now, and think how many happy wives, mothers, and sweethearts there will be.*

The next day, Frank also responded to the news reports by writing her:

> *Guess by now you've heard the big news about Russia declaring war on Japan. The last week has really brought tremendous news. First the "atomic bomb" and then yesterday Russia's declaration of war. I think the world is now just sitting on the edge of its seat waiting to see what is going to happen. I heard over the radio a few moments ago that a second atomic bomb had been dropped on Japan. I can't see them lasting more than a few months at the most. Maybe I'm just overly optimistic, but I feel better about the war now than at any time since I've been in the army.*

The world had to wait five more days after the atomic bomb dropped on Nagasaki for Japanese leaders to acknowledge that there was no path forward. Finally, Emperor Hirohito came to grips with the reality of his country's situation and agreed to surrender unconditionally. He wrote one of the classic understatements of all times: *The war situation has developed not necessarily to Japan's advantage.* World War II was over!

Now, on that August Tuesday, in her dorm in Southwest Missouri, Iris again turned to paper. She had to share this moment with Frank and wrote in pencil:

It is over! Horns and sirens have been going all over town. I don't feel like horn blowing but I feel wonderful though. I couldn't find my fountain pen but maybe you can read this. Maybe these letters will soon be things of the past. You are coming home, Honey!

Frank was on night guard duty when he heard the news. Back in his barracks the next morning, he too reached for a pen and paper to write her. Their letters crossed in the mail.

Sugar, at last that day for which we've been praying and hoping so much has arrived. Yesterday evening, we had just gone on guard when the news came through. There had been rumors all day on the radio that peace was imminent, but when nothing had come through, most of us thought it would be today. At shortly after six, every whistle, bell, and siren within hearing distance tore loose. Even a train traveling down the track was bellowing its whistle and ringing its bell. It was a glorious feeling. A good feeling of thanksgiving was in most of our minds. Everyone now has sort of returned to normal, and we are carrying on as usual. This morning there was a Thanksgiving service, and wherever it is possible men are taking it easy for the day.

It is rather difficult to say at present just what the army will be like. It will probably be quite a while before any great changes at most are made. At least now we can see a light

*where there was only darkness before. This should mark the
beginning of a long era of peace; at least we hope so.*

It was not until September 2, 1945, that the treaty ending
World War II was signed. For Frank, it was "*the day we should be
most thankful for in our lives.*" Every person who had ever lived
in the Show-Me State, from President Truman on down, was
especially proud that the ceremony in Tokyo Bay took place
on the USS *Missouri*. The great ship built for war became
an altar to peace, as General Douglas MacArthur formally
accepted the Japanese surrender.

Soon, the amount of guard duty required by Frank's unit
was reduced. The ships coming through the canal were no
longer a threat. On October 8, Frank watched as eighteen
warships, taking more than 56,000 navy and army veterans
home from the Pacific, passed through the Panama Canal. It
was an emotional sight for Frank and the other G.I.s who
cheered their arrival. Bands on shore and on the deck of the
ships played Souza marches and the Star-Spangled Banner.
Frank cheered even louder a few days later when the huge
battleship *Missouri*, barely fitting through the locks, came
through the canal on its route from Tokyo Bay to New York,
and to victory celebrations with President Truman.

The planners in Washington, D.C., had the difficult job of
bringing all those men stationed around the world home in
an orderly fashion. They worked out a point system to give
priority to men who had been away the longest and who
saw extensive combat. American soldiers in Panama were
moved to the back of the line in terms of coming home. But
these men had to be kept busy and out of trouble. Frank was
asked to volunteer (although in the army, one did not truly
volunteer) to teach classes in agricultural chemistry, livestock
management, and other subjects, to help prepare the men

for civilian life. It was now Iris's turn to encourage him as a teacher.

These men knew that there were veteran's benefits waiting for them. Ten months before he died, President Roosevelt signed the Servicemen's Readjustment Act of 1944, known commonly as the G.I. Bill. Americans felt they owed much to these men who had put their lives on hold to fight for their country. The bill offered the returning veteran money for college tuition, a loan guaranty for a home, farm, or business, and unemployment pay. The men in Frank's classes in Panama wanted to get a head start on civilian life. They lined up to take his classes. At night, Frank wrote letters of recommendation to colleges for his fellow soldiers, including some who were not in his classes. And after these official letters, he always wrote Iris.

Iris was now back home in Dade County. Her last summer session at Southwest Baptist College was over. It was time to get ready for her new school year. The county had moved her to the Star School, where she received little support from the local school board and the parents. She spent her first week home cleaning the school and getting it ready for the fall opening. She also had to make a trip to a neighboring town to procure needed supplies and books. She was teaching all grades.

> *I have four new students Monday morning. I'm in a worse shape for books than I was before I picked up books Saturday. I have seventeen in school now. I have four in the first grade, one in the second, four in the third, one in the fourth, one in the fifth, and three in the sixth, now two in the seventh and one in the eighth. Quite different from the one [school] I had last year.*

The new students are all way behind the rest of my kids, so I have to have special classes for them.

She wrote her frustrations to Frank in her letters to him each night. Sometimes with the morning light, she felt more positive and tore up the letter before she sent it. She did not want to burden him with her problems. She tried to stay focused on the present and on her students. But at times it was hard not to think about the future. Frank would be coming home and she knew they would be married. It was an excitement that Iris shared with all her girlfriends. They were all engaged and planning weddings. Each had picked out a china and silver pattern. One cynic among her friends remarked that "it was a fad to be engaged." Iris did not want a big wedding. Her dreams centered on making a home for Frank and on the children that they would create together. But she did pick out a silver pattern. When she had a few extra dollars that year, she bought an individual silver spoon or fork.

Frank's letters changed when the military censors stopped reading the outgoing mail. Panama was so different than rural Missouri. It was a world of alligators, the San Blas Indians, and extreme poverty among the local population. He described the colonialism of the Canal Zone and the discrimination and the disparity in incomes:

> *The natives have to exist someway and in order to live they will do anything. The white people who live here are just the opposite. They have large well-built homes that will have an average value of $25,000. They live in the suburbs of the city and they live well.*

He knew the military presence was a boon to the local economy and worried about what would happen when the soldiers left. He also shared the beauty of the land:

It has been nice here today. The afternoon got pretty tiresome, but the six hours finally passed. I wish you could see some of the effects that the sun and moon can produce around here on the water and vegetation. Particularly at night. I've never seen anywhere the mystic effect that is produced here by the moonlight on the waters of the lake and the trees round it. It reminds you very much of some of the descriptions you read of the Scottish lowlands. It is exceptionally nice. It just seems like a quivering haze is over everything.

I like to describe these places to you so much. I hope you like to read about them. The thing missing however is the noise of the insects and frogs and such that you hear there at home. Everything here just seems to hold its breath and stand still. There is one old frog who comes around near where I am at night sometimes and he must be dumb for he never has even uttered a sound. Just seems to sit there and stare with large reproachful eyes at me for invading his domain. I've tried talking to him sometimes, but that doesn't seem to bother him very much. Maybe that sounds queer but that's a fair description of what the place is sort of like.

Iris was again living with her parents and eagerly awaited the mail each day. She loved his descriptions of the tropical land and read the especially descriptive passages aloud to her mother, Carrie. His prose allowed them to picture a land so different than rural Southwest Missouri. Through Frank's eyes and words, their world expanded. Neither Iris nor her mother would ever visit a foreign country. When she was an old woman, Carrie regretted not having seen the world. In 1964, she wrote:

I always thought I would like to travel, but I have not education enough to make it enjoyable.

Frank's letters brought Panama and its people to the tarpaper shack in the Ozarks. Iris felt that Frank allowed her to know "pretty well what they are like." She wrote him:

> *Honey, it won't be long until you will have been in Panama a year. I am glad that if you had to be in the army, and we had to have this war, that you have had the opportunity to see a part of the world.*

Frank sent Iris a purse made by native hands, decorated with large tropical flowers. Iris had never had anything so exotic. He visited ancient relics, always carrying a camera. He spent much of his spare time creating a photo album to share with her when he returned home. Their excitement grew with each letter, as they knew they would soon see each other.

On November 16, 1945, Frank wrote that his major just told him that his unit was the next group scheduled to leave the Isthmus. He would be home for Christmas. It was the last letter that Frank wrote to Iris from Panama. She put this one in the special box where she kept all his letters. By then, it held almost two hundred letters. Most of them were over three pages. She fantasized that she and Frank would read them together on an anniversary sometime in the future.

Iris and Frank made plans. He was to call the Old Sylvania General Store as soon as he arrived in the states, since the McClueys did not have a telephone. Someone would send for her, and they would hear each other's voices. He wanted Iris to "meet me in St. Louis," as the popular movie title suggested. But Finn vetoed that idea. He did not like the image of his unmarried daughter traveling across the state to meet a solider. Iris was living under her father's roof and rules. So she waited for Frank to return home.

On November 26, 1945, Frank Sweaney was officially discharged from the army at the Jefferson Barracks in St. Louis. He headed home to the Ozarks and to his girl. Finn tried to persuade the young couple to spend some time together before they got married. This time Iris and Frank stood their ground. They did not intend to wait any longer than absolutely necessary. They had been separated long enough.

On Saturday, December 22, 1945, less than a month after Frank was discharged from the army, Iris McCluey and Frank Sweaney were married.

Frank and Iris's wedding day

Frank is still tan from his service in Panama.

My Treasures Are Laid Up Somewhere Beyond the Blue

Twenty-Six

Harry Truman loved symbolic details. He staged items on his desk in the Oval Office carefully. During the war, he placed a miniature cannon next to his famous "The buck stops here" sign. In 1946, he replaced the cannon with a small plow. The men coming in droves to study at the University of Missouri in Columbia that winter may once have been farm boys behind the plow. Now they were men who did not see a plow in their future. They sought a job with an income that would take them far away from the hardships of their teenage years. Technology and science helped win the war, and these disciplines were seen as America's future. The University of Missouri's engineering and medical schools soon were full.

These veterans, eager to take advantage of the G.I. Bill, changed the face of the university. They did not have time for the games of the college freshmen and did not expect immediate success. Most had lived through hard times before the war and knew that nothing came without work. But it was different now. They were working not just to survive, but for a dream. There was often a new bride beside these men. If nothing else, the war years also taught these women to accept delayed gratification.

This was the world where Frank and Iris began their married life. They arrived in the college town of Columbia less than a month after their marriage ceremony. The town was bursting at the seams. Returning veterans were everywhere. The town and the university were unprepared for this influx of students and wives. According to school records, there were only 2,136 total students enrolled the previous winter term that started January of 1945. Now, as the country settled into peacetime, the university saw its enrollment jump to 5,915 students. The next fall, the university administration had to make room for 10,383 students, with 6,709 of them being returning veterans.

The lack of housing reached a crisis level. Columbia did not have enough rooms for all the students arriving to study, and so the university bought surplus buildings from the U.S. military. Modular barracks, Quonset huts, and trailers were set up on the edge of the campus. The accommodations were not luxurious, but the veterans were used to such quarters. Frank and Iris put their names on the waiting list for a trailer, but they had to have a place to live in the meantime. Frank's medical school classes were about to begin.

In desperation, Frank went to talk to Mrs. Creed, his former landlady. Her husband lost everything in the stock market crash of 1929 and killed himself rather than face his losses. She turned her home on Rosemary Lane into a men's boarding house in order to survive. It was Frank's *home away from home* before the war, and Mrs. Creed had mothered him. He took his bride to meet her and explained that they needed some place to live. Mrs. Creed came to their rescue and offered them a basement room in Creed House.

Iris was the only woman tenant in the place. It presented some unique challenges for her. She wrote to her older sister in February 1946:

There are four boys and Frank and I here in the basement.
It makes me feel a little queer never to see a girl here, but I
like it here. The boys are nice, friendly boys.

It was not easy to set up housekeeping. The basement room was not meant for a couple, and there was not much money to spare. Lingering wartime shortages meant that it was impossible to find basic items. Iris wrote home to her mother:

I never have found very much stuff to keep house with. I
couldn't find a dish pan or a very large pan. I have to wash
dishes in a small kettle and wash pan. I don't have any way
of keeping the numerous mice and coal dirt out of my dishes,
so they have to be washed often, whether they are used or
not. I can't get a rolling pin or potato masher or anything like
that. Maybe they won't always be so hard to get.

The benefits of the G.I. Bill often did not adequately cover the expenses of the new families. Like many of the young couples, both Iris and Frank had to work to make ends meet while he continued his education. She found a part-time job, and he worked about twenty hours a week in addition to his classes.

This story was repeated across America's college campuses and was reflected in popular culture. Hollywood focused on the new college experience in movies such as *Apartment for Peggy* (starring William Holden and Jeanne Crain), where a returning veteran and his pregnant wife are forced to live in an attic of a retired professor. A few years later, when the story shifted to the need for houses for the new families, and America entered a housing crisis, movies such as *Miss Grant Takes Richmond* (where Lucille Ball becomes a real estate developer) became popular.

In his first medical school class, Frank learned the art of suturing. The future doctors practiced on cats. After sewing up a different cat during several sessions, he came up with a time saving idea as a joke. He and his lab mate decided that it would be much more efficient if they sewed a zipper into the cat's belly; that way they could examine the cat's organs with ease. His buddies took a picture of Frank in front of the cat with the zipper. You could see his neat stiches. They rivaled his mother-in-law's needle work. Later, he was recognized by his peers as a gifted surgeon.

Iris supported him in any way possible. Frank called his wife one day and told her to meet him at the pathology department. She did not realize that this meant the morgue. He handed her his textbook and asked her to read aloud marked pages while he worked; however, she did not understand the full meaning of "while I work." When he pulled out a cadaver and started dissecting it, she fainted!

The couple stretched each dollar as Iris worried over where they would find money for the necessities of life. When Frank needed new shoes, they scraped together the money for him to buy a new pair. Frank wore them for the first time when he attended the wedding of a good friend. When he and Iris arrived, the groom was in a panic. He had left his good shoes at home. Being the great friend that he was, Frank took off his new shoes and handed them over to the nervous groom to wear. By the time the groom finished pacing back and forth before the ceremony, Frank's new shoes were broken in.

In spite of the lack of material goods, Iris was happy. By summer, their names moved to the top of the waiting list for married student housing, and they moved into a trailer. Iris and Frank had their first home. Slowly, she bought small items. One of those items, a special dishtowel, caused their first fight. Although she had little money, a pretty inexpensive towel caught her eye, and she treated herself. The towel was just what she needed to add color to the trailer's small kitchen. She hung it by the sink. Frank came in dirty and a little greasy and grabbed the towel in order to clean up.

Iris yelled at him, "That towel is not to be used. It is to be pretty!" She stormed out of the trailer.

Frank was a little surprised, as he had never seen her angry.

Later, Iris apologized. "I am sorry that I got so mad at you."

Frank answered with a twinkle in his eyes. "Were you angry? I didn't notice."

What could she do but laugh, and with that, their first fight was over.

One day, Frank brought home a cage with three cute white mice in it. He told Iris that he could use them for medical experiments. Iris just looked at him. She knew that the playful rodents soon would be pets. She found a place for the cage in the trailer. She fed them each morning, and there was no more talk of medical experiments.

Soon after the mice, Teddy came to live with them. He had four paws, a big pink tongue, and perhaps a little Collie in him. He went everywhere with the couple that summer, even to the Dairy Queen. Teddy always got his own cone.

Iris and Frank were not the only Americans enjoying ice cream that summer. In 1946, the cold treat was all the rage, and Americans purchased 714 million gallons of ice cream that year.

That fall, Iris had the chance to return to teaching. Although she had taken a few classes at the university, they made Frank's education the priority; her college degree could wait. This decision was expedient at the time, but would greatly affect her life later. They needed the income, and the one-room Vawter School outside of Columbia needed a teacher. Boone County, where Columbia and the Vawter School were located, was much more prosperous than Dade County, where she had taught before. She could not believe it when she signed the contract. She was to be paid $125 a month, which almost tripled the amount she had received from her first teaching contract. The Vawter students were eager to learn, and she was glad to be able to return to them in 1947. Years later, she found a picture in her box of memories of a small wooden building. She was posed in front of it with her students. She wrote on it, *Vawter School, precious memories.*

The University of Missouri only offered the first two years of medical training. By the summer of 1948, Frank had learned everything offered in Columbia and needed to transfer to another school in order to become a doctor. He was admitted to the University of Tennessee College of Medicine in Memphis.

Frank and Iris packed up their few belongings and moved to a large city for the first and only time in their married life. Before they left, they returned the mice to the lab. That was not hard to do. But Iris had tears in her eyes when they said goodbye to Teddy. They sent him back to Dade County to live with Frank's parents. He was not meant to be a city dog.

Twenty-Seven

Americans were leaving the Great Depression and the sacrifices of the war years behind. A new America was emerging, where optimism was taking hold. Finn McCluey felt it. In 1948, he drove his car to the bank, wrote out a check, and gave it to the bank manager. It was his final payment on his mortgage. The McCluey land was free and clear.

On his way home, Finn felt free from the tension and anxiety that had hung over him for almost twenty years. He felt the need to share this feeling with his wife, Carrie. He bought her a fancy mirror so that she could see herself as others saw her. She was always so tidy and arranged her hair so carefully each day. She hung it above the washstand in her kitchen; the family called it their "celebration mirror." Although they were now free of much of their financial anxiety, Finn and Carrie continued to live as they had before. Finn did not upgrade his home to include electricity and indoor plumbing.

Finn and Carrie, out of debt

Although the McCluey land was free and clear, Finn and Carrie did not upgrade their house or change their standard of living.

At sixty-four, Carrie found a new role as grandmother. Escaping an unhappy marriage, her oldest daughter, Gwendolyn, came home that year with three small children. Carrie bonded with the youngest, a two and a half-year-old named Elaine. While the two older children attended school and Gwen worked days at a local nursing home, Grandma Carrie took care of Elaine. For the next several years, she gave Gwen's youngest constant love and attention. Carrie encouraged the child to draw, as she had done many years before. She brought out her own drawing books that she created before she was married. Elaine used her grandmother's sketchbooks as coloring books and filled in the beautiful sketches with Crayola. The two drew on paper bags, since there was no drawing paper in the house. Elaine tried to mimic the drawing techniques Carrie showed her on the brown paper. The magazines that Carrie had collected over the years were now used to create a family of paper dolls, dressed in clothing that showed influences from the prior three decades.

Carrie's role as grandmother was to expand. While Frank was completing his medical training, Iris found herself pregnant. She was not alone. Everyone was having babies. More babies were born in 1946 than ever before, and this increase continued almost until the mid-1960s. In *Great Expectations: America and the Baby Boom Generation,* historian Landon Jones noted that almost exactly nine months after World War II ended, "the cry of the baby was heard across the land." In 1949, Iris and Frank's first daughter, Lou Ann, was one of 3.56 million babies born that year.

During her pregnancy, Iris found herself far away from home and knew few people in the big city. She was alone much of the time. When not in formal classes, Frank spent hours rotating through various duty assignments at Baptist Memorial Hospital. When he came home, no matter what time it was, they had long talks into the night. He shared details of his day with her. His enthusiasm for his work and his humor always made her feel better. He always told her some interesting story of a patient or a detail that he had just learned. He made her smile. These conversations always helped her suppress her anxieties. With Frank by her side, she knew that everything would work out. The little baby growing inside her was evidence of their love for each other. She spent her time preparing for the new baby and making baby clothes from any material she could find.

She wrote to her sisters often. They had always been best friends. Some passages from a letter written to Gwen in

February 1949 capture her life as the pregnant wife of a doctor in training:

Frank is on OB tonight. I don't know whether he'll get home during the night or not. He surprised me by coming to the doctor's office while I was there this morning. He said there were just two students ahead of him at 10:30 this morning, so he could come in any time, but he may not get here at all tonight.

I am going to have to have some new clothes soon. I thought I wouldn't need them until April, but I will. I want to get a pattern before I try to cut my dresses. I have made a little nightgown and four little undershirts. One of the undershirts is made from the tails of one of Frank's old shirts. He says he may come home and find I have cut up all of his shirts for baby clothes. (ha) The others are made of some material I bought for blouses when we lived in Columbia. The gown is made from the tails of a gown I bought last winter. We have bought one little underskirt. I have a blanket that Frank bought for me over a year ago. He said he would buy me a pair of pink and white booties for my Valentine present, but I expect that will have to wait a few days, as we are out of money at present. I believe the clothes made from old material will wear all right on a young baby. I have a pink skirt I am going to make a dress from and I have enough material for about three underskirts, then I want to get some new material.

I rather overdid the thing yesterday so today I'm not doing so much. I did a washing yesterday before going to the doctor and cleaned the house. I got up a little after five but I rushed to get it all done, as I had to be there at 10:30. I have to walk over half a mile to the bus line and I hurried. The doctor's examination made me sore so I'm taking life easy today. I do have to do my ironing.

Iris did not think of her own needs. She felt that it was her role to stretch each dollar and take care of the practical matters. Frank was never the one to worry about money and was willing to spend it when necessary. He was optimistic and confident that life would work out. She was relieved that her doctor did not charge medical students or their wives and tried to push aside her worry about the hospital bill that would come when her baby was delivered. On August 17, 1949, Lou Ann Sweaney came into the world.

Frank and Iris, like other baby boom parents, wanted to protect their children from hardship. They turned to science and new methods to give their children a better start. Instead of relying on child-rearing advice from her mother, Carrie, and other older women, Iris, like other post-war mothers, turned to a book by an East Coast pediatrician for guidance. Dr. Benjamin Spock's *Common Sense Book of Baby and Child Care* was first published in 1946, but continued to sell almost a million copies each year during the baby boom years. Dr. Spock emphasized that mothers needed to use their instincts. In Spock's world, child care was the mother's responsibility, and the father's role was minimized. The father was to earn the living and the mother was to take care of the home and children. Spock abandoned the old "spare the rod and spoil the child" axiom that marked child-rearing for children for generations.

Not only were there new theories on child care, but also there were new ideas on the healthiest way to feed children. Commercial formulas and pre-processed baby food became big business. As a marketing strategy to encourage the use of their products, baby food companies offered free samples to doctors to share with their patients. As a medical student, Frank received complimentary samples of commercial baby food for this purpose, which proved to be a godsend. He made very little money, but he was able to eat most of his meals at the hospital. Iris did not have this option, so she ate the strained fruit and vegetables along with her little girl.

The next May, Iris held a squirming Lou Ann on her lap as she watched Frank Sweaney walk across the stage at the University of Tennessee College of Medicine's graduation ceremony. Against all odds, the boy who had walked to high school because he could not afford to ride the bus was now Dr. I.F. Sweaney.

Twenty-Eight

The soldiers, sailors, and airmen had been home from the war for five years. The many veterans who had taken advantage of the G.I. Bill were now graduating and entering their communities as productive citizens with growing families. This flood of new talent was driving the country into an era of prosperity and plenty that contrasted greatly with the poverty and worries of the previous two decades. We had fought and won the "good war" and it was now time to reap the benefits. Although there were tensions caused by rising international rivalries, the fear of communism, and the budding civil rights struggles, the mood was generally optimistic. As Andrew J. Dunar wrote in *America in the Fifties*:

> *If ever people living in the United States had reason to believe that theirs was the American Century, it was during the 1950s. The United States came out of World War II not only one of the most powerful nations in human history, but also one of the most affluent.*

Frank Sweaney was part of this wave of trained and educated veterans. He completed his medical training by spending another year as an intern at Baptist Memorial Hospital in Memphis. Despite the long hours and little sleep, the year worked out well for him. Iris was alone with an active baby most of the time, since Frank was only home about twelve out of every sixty hours. Frank and Iris were products of their times, and Iris did not question her role. It was *how it was done*.

By earning the right to put MD after his name, Frank was entering an elite group. The emphasis on science, along with the advent of antibiotics and successful treatments, pushed the medical profession to new heights of prestige that peaked during 1960s. Iris and Frank visited the land of their childhood, and the McCluey family gathered together to greet them. The McClueys had always worked hard, but never had achieved material or worldly success. They were tremendously proud of Frank. It meant something to have a doctor in the family.

Frank, Iris, and Lou Ann return to the Ozarks

The McCluey family came out to greet Dr. Sweaney and his wife. They were very proud to have a doctor in the family.

At the end of his internship, Frank and Iris made a decision: they both wanted to return to Missouri. Iris was adamant that she did not want to go back to the Ozarks. Frank applied for a surgical residency at Missouri Methodist Hospital in St. Joseph, a small city of around eighty thousand in the Northwest corner of the state. Not only could he continue his career, but Iris's sister Avis had settled in St. Joe. He came well recommended.

On August 9, 1951, Dr. Frank S. Groner, the administrator at Baptist Memorial wrote Frank:

> *We are in the process of sending intern evaluation to the deans of various medical schools, and I am pleased to report to you that you ranked very high.*
>
> *It is not our custom to advise interns of their rank, but because of a notation which was made on a number of your evaluations, I am sending this note to you to express my appreciation of your fine work as an intern.*
>
> *Incidentally, of the thirty men evaluated, you ranked first in chart work.*

Frank got the position. Iris, Frank, and their very active toddler headed back to the "Show-Me" state. When they left Tennessee behind and moved to St. Joseph, they also were leaving behind the poverty and hardscrabble life of the Ozarks. The economy of their new home was based on the fertile farmland along the banks of the Missouri River, very different from the rocky soil of the Ozarks.

Lou Ann Sweaney as a toddler

Lou Ann never stood still for long.

Frank and Iris settled into a new routine. She was kept busy trying to keep up with Lou Ann, who was always moving. She spent time with her sister Avis and her two small children, Larry and Marilyn. Frank was at the hospital much of the time, but they were able to develop a life together. They joined the Baptist Church, where they found other married couples with young children. They were all of the same age, and most of the men were veterans. They understood each other. Frank loved to be around people, and they socialized with these couples. As the calendar turned a page to the year 1952, Iris found herself pregnant with her second child.

It was not a bad life, but Iris and Frank knew it was not permanent. Frank wanted a practice of his own in a small town.

Twenty-Nine

In the spring of 1952, the Missouri River flooded. The swollen river cut a destructive path through the seven states that make up the river basin. The powerful muddy water spread out across America's heartland, spreading fifteen miles wide in some places. The "Big Muddy" destroyed land and homes as it moved south, leaving mud and heartbreak in its wake. Water was everywhere. Not only did the Missouri leave its banks, but small tributaries such as the Nodaway also flooded. Bridges between Missouri and neighboring Kansas and Nebraska collapsed. In St. Joe, houses were covered with water, and some homes were destroyed beyond repair. Medical professionals, trying to prevent an epidemic, were kept busy administering typhoid shots. Frank had to work long hours at the hospital in response to the crisis.

Holt County, Missouri, located thirty miles up the river from St. Joe, was hit hard. The river serves as the natural boundary between the county and the neighboring states of Kansas and Nebraska. The land nestled along the river is fertile, and the county's economy is based on this rich soil. That spring, farmers were exhausted trying to hold the river back by strategically placing sandbags. An entire growing season was lost. They worried about the muck that would be left on their fields if and when the waters receded. Then the Missouri River showed its independent personality. It did not want to return to its former channel. The river cut a new path, redrawing borders between the three states. Everyone in the county, even those who lived inland from the river, was affected. Roads were impassable, and Oregon, the county seat, was cut off from the rest of the world.

Famers gathered in Oregon and gossiped over coffee. They compared notes on the rising water and talked about events of the day. In addition to the flood, everyone was concerned about old Doc Kearney. He was getting ready to retire, and people wondered what they would do without a doctor. Jim Fitzgerald, the Holt County tax collector, heard an interesting piece of news: a young doctor in St. Joe wanted to practice in a small town. Jim talked to Melvin Scheib, another prominent citizen. Melvin owned Scheib's Hardware, the commercial center of the small town. The two community leaders came up with a plan. Oregon needed a doctor. If they could just talk with the young physician, they knew they could convince him that Oregon was the town for him; however, they could not reach him by car. All the roads between Holt County and St. Joseph were under water.

So they took a boat and traveled down the bloated river, crossing flooded farmland and water-covered roads to make it to St. Joe to meet with Frank Sweaney. They told the young man of their hometown and how it needed a doctor. They explained that there were plenty of patients that needed his attention. The school was good and it was a great place to raise a family. Melvin added that there was a building right on the town square that was perfect for a doctor's office. At thirty-two, Frank was eager to settle down. He was done with his training and was ready to create a medical practice of his own. He was a country boy at heart and done with the city. It sounded like a good fit.

Iris was a little disappointed when she and Frank approached Oregon the first time. It was May, still the wrong time of year to see the small town, as the leaves on the trees were still budding. Oregon is always at its best in mid-June, before the heat sets in, or in the fall, when the leaves turn yellow and orange. The drive from St. Joe had not been pretty. Water had receded so that the road was passable, but the river left behind devastation. Approaching the town on old Highway 59, it initially seemed that there was nothing to it. It was about the same size Iris's hometown, Lockwood; however, she relaxed once she saw the town square. The majestic old courthouse was surrounded by large trees that gave a look of prosperity and stability.

Oregon, Missouri, was like many small towns that dotted the landscape of rural America in the 1950s. The region's economy was based on farming. Only about eight hundred people actually lived within the town limits, but it served as the commercial center for the farm families who lived on the rich land that surrounded the town. The residents of the area claimed that the "Missouri River bottom land in Holt County was some of the richest farmland in the world." It was a self-contained community. Around the square were a hardware store, four grocery stores, two banks, a furniture store, law offices, and a tavern. Oregon was the county seat, and the elected officials in the courthouse were mostly Republicans.

Frank and Iris stopped their car on the southwest corner of the town square. They looked at the small building that Melvin said would make a good doctor's office. It was just a few buildings down from his hardware store. When they walked in the door, Frank could picture a waiting room. To the side was a perfect room for a desk and an examining table, and behind that room was a kitchen with a closet that he could modify to a darkroom, where he could develop X-rays. Down the hallway were a bathroom and another room to house the big X-ray machine that someday he would have the money to buy. He could picture it. His mind was full of his plans, and he thought this building would work out just fine.

So, it was decided. This was where Frank wanted to practice medicine. It was Frank's dream, shared by Iris: a medical practice of his own. They had worked hard to get to this point. It was a dream first articulated in letters that flowed between Panama and the Ozarks during the war. It was nurtured through sacrifice in Columbia and Memphis. The dream was spoken aloud during long talks into the night. Missouri Methodist was just a pit stop along the path toward this dream.

Where his growing family would live was of secondary importance. They found living quarters in a large Victorian-era white clapboard house about five blocks from the office building. It had already seen better days. It was built in 1910 and had the interesting design features of its time. It was large, with bay windows, high ceilings, and beautiful woodwork. Frank and Iris would call it home for the rest of their married life. It officially sat at 600 West Pine Street. But no one in the small community relied on house numbers. Not even the mailman identified the houses by the street numbers. The house sat on a pretty corner lot, with plenty of room for Lou Ann to play in the large yard. It would work out just fine. Iris was almost six months pregnant now and wanted to be settled before the next baby came. They signed papers and made plans to move to the town in two months.

In the meantime, there were details to handle, such as putting together an office staff. Frank bought a physician's daily record book to keep track of his patients. He was a little nervous. Would anyone really visit the office that he was setting up? He ordered a telephone and was assigned the number 14. Of course, patients had to go through the telephone operator to reach him. He would soon find that most people did not ask for "Number 14."Instead, they just asked the operator to connect them to the new doctor.

While Frank set up his office, Iris prepared to move to a new home. She officially took up residence on the first day of July in the heat of a Missouri summer. She was in her new yard a week later when she felt the first pain. She thought, *It's too early. The baby is not due for at least another month.* But regardless, I was ready to be born.

Iris had not yet met the neighbor who was pulling weeds in her yard but said to her, "I think I am going to have a baby."

Mrs. Fansher looked at her and said, "Well, I guess you should call the doctor."

Frank took her to Missouri Methodist in St. Joe. She had been seeing one of his friends for her maternity care. It was a difficult delivery, requiring an unplanned caesarean section. In addition to other problems, my mother's inherited RH negative blood meant that her body tried to reject my foreign blood type. Unlike Iris's baby sister Winnifred June, I had the benefit of what was called "modern medicine" in 1952. A few months later, my mother took me to see this doctor. He held me, looked at my mother, and said, "I thought we were going to lose both of you that night."

Iris returned to the big white house with a new baby that seemed to cry all the time. She knew no one in the community. Oregon had few newcomers in 1952. People in Holt County not only knew each other well, they also were probably related. Their roots went back generations. It was a safe bet that a person had someone by the name of Markt or Kurtz in their family tree. So people knew who Iris was even if she did not yet know who they were.

Thirty

Iris was now a doctor's wife. In the 1950s, that phrase conjured up images promoted by popular culture. Doctors' wives were seen as part of America's new affluent middle class. Veteran movie star Donna Reed moved to the small screen with a popular TV show bearing her name. In it, she was Donna Stone, the wife of a pediatrician. It was set in Hillsdale, a mythical small city somewhere in the Midwest. The episodes revolved around an idealized family, with Donna engaged in community activities and charity drives. Like June Cleaver, Beaver's mom in *Leave it to Beaver*, Donna often did housework wearing a pearl necklace and high heels. Dr. Alex Stone still made house calls, but he was found at home in most episodes and had time for social activities. This had little resemblance to the life that Iris soon led. As was the case since the beginning of their marriage, her schedule always revolved around Frank's. Her role was to support him and rear her children, while Frank's focus was first and foremost on his patients.

She began to find her place in her new community. On a Sunday morning a few weeks after I was born, Iris walked into the First Christian Church for the first time, carrying me in her arms and holding Lou Ann's hand. Despite its small size, Oregon was the home to four large churches. Institutional religion thrived in America after World War II. People felt that God was on America's side and was rewarding us. Across the country, in small towns and large cities, churches were filled on Sundays. During the decade, church attendance rose. By 1960, sixty-nine percent of Americans claimed to be church members, which was the highest level in the twentieth century. Most Protestant churches displayed the American flag in their sanctuaries and had plaques memorializing those who had given their lives for their country. In Oregon, as well as in much of America, King James and Uncle Sam were considered to be related.

In Oregon, churches not only provided a place to worship, but also a place for people to meet and hold events. Potluck dinners, bake sales, and chili suppers brought people together almost as often as the weekly services. Youth groups and vacation Bible school provided activities for growing families. Generations of a family often attended the same church. There was an Oregon tradition that a girl was married in her family's church, but then would attend her husband's family's church after the marriage ceremony. People chose to attend church for many reasons beyond denominational practices; however, not yet being a part of the social network, Iris chose the First Christian Church because it was the closest she could find to the Baptist church of her youth.

That first Sunday, Iris sat in a pew on the north side of the church. It only took a few more Sundays for this to become *her* pew. She joined others her age in the BBC (Build Better Christians) class. Over the next forty years, she taught this group on a regular basis. The minister of the church, Merrill Ferguson, and his wife, Berniece, became close friends. Merrill, like Frank, loved to talk and swap stories. On most Sunday evenings, the Fergusons would stop by for dinner at the Sweaneys. Very soon, Frank became a deacon in the church, but this was not in honor of his regular church attendance. More often than not, he was with a patient on Sunday mornings. It ultimately might have been better if he had used the Sabbath as a "day of rest."

Iris was asked to join several of the women's social clubs. Although she was never a true "club-woman," she did join several. These women met over coffee and tea, gossiped, and discussed their children. They planned civic activities, raised money for a new park in Oregon, and helped in the constant effort to fight polio through the March of Dimes. It was a source of pride that when a woman hosted a club meeting, she made a special dessert and served it on her best dishes.

World War II was fresh in people's memories, and most men of Frank's age were veterans. The American Legion and the Veterans of Foreign Wars (VFW) competed for members. Iris found like-minded friends in the Ladies Auxiliary of the American Legion. These women focused on education programs, and Iris felt at home with them. She soon found herself chairing the annual Poppy Poster Contest, which raised awareness and funds for Veteran's hospitals. School children designed large posters with pictures of poppies and patriotic messages. These posters were displayed in storefronts around the courthouse square. The posters were judged, and red, white, and blue ribbons were placed on the winners. Around Memorial Day, the auxiliary handed out red crepe paper poppies. They weren't sold, but people understood that a donation was expected. The poppies had a metal stem that could be wrapped around a button on a shirt or blouse and worn proudly. Of course, there was a difference between the poppies distributed by the American Legion and the "rival" VFW. The Legion poppies were made of crepe paper, unlike the VFW's stiff red Buddy Poppies.

Although Frank wore the poppy proudly, he did not have the time to engage in civic activities. He was ready to contribute financially to a cause, but his time was always committed. His worry about having no patients was unfounded, as there were constant emergencies and, in these baby-boom times, babies to deliver. As the only MD in the county for much of the decade, he was always on call. Within six months of settling in Oregon, his office was always crowded.

Frank's daily record book for 1953 shows a stream of patients every day. Sundays and holidays were no exception. On July 4, while other people were celebrating Independence Day, he saw twenty-four people in his office. On Christmas Day, which fell on a Friday that year, he saw only thirteen patients, but that Saturday, sixty-seven people who had put off seeking medical attention while celebrating Christmas showed up. That Sunday, twenty-eight people came to his office.

Doc Sweaney with a patient

Frank Sweaney listened intently to his patients. It was one of the reasons they loved him so much.

Every day, including weekends, Frank left home at six a.m. to drive forty miles, each way, to do hospital rounds in a small hospital in Fairfax, Missouri. After his office closed, he then went on house calls, usually driving more than a hundred miles each night.

Soon, people commented that Doc "just worked all the time and needed to take more time for himself," but they still called him at four-thirty in the morning. He saw the people's needs, and there was something in him that did not allow him to say no. By the end of the decade, his workload significantly increased, as people came to see him not only from Holt and neighboring counties in Missouri, but even from the adjoining states of Kansas and Nebraska. People loved him for his dedication, concern, his sense of humor, and his charisma.

Not all the situations were true emergencies, as one of Frank's office workers remembered half a century later:

> I worked for your dad in the office for two weeks when Pat Key (his receptionist) was on vacation. I remember one call I took and relayed to your dad. The person called saying they had been poisoned. Your dad insisted that they get to the office right away. When they got there, it was a case of poison ivy.

In no time at all, the Sweaney family was an integral part of the close-knit Oregon community. There were few people in town who did not have a "Doc Sweaney" story to tell. He had delivered their babies, taken out their tonsils, set their broken bones, and listened to their woes. Covers of the *Saturday Evening Post* often featured Norman

Rockwell illustrations depicting family doctors who came day or night, rain or shine, to heal the sick and console the dying. Frank had one of these illustrations framed and hung on his office wall. For Doc Sweaney, this was not a myth. Perhaps if he had set true office hours, taken Sundays as a "day of rest," or Thursday afternoons off to play golf like city doctors often did, then his story might have ended differently.

His wife was always in the background, and she, along with his office staff, made it possible for him to handle his incredible patient load. After his staff left for the day, Iris brought her small children to the office while he saw more patients. She acted as his receptionist and clerk. She comforted the patients waiting to see him and sometimes held their hands during a procedure. After he closed his doors, there were always house calls to make. Even family time on Sunday afternoons revolved around these home visits. If people needing medical attention saw Doc's car in his home driveway any time, day or night, they felt free to knock on the door for care. In essence, the clapboard house was an extension of his office.

The Sweaney family life revolved around Frank's medical practice. It was not that his family didn't see him; his family went to him. Family meals were usually consumed on the go at a restaurant, because seldom was there time for the family to sit down to dinner at home. Iris treasured any time with her husband, and said many years later, "If I would not have gone on house calls, I would not have seen him."

Iris, Debby, and Lou Ann in Frank's office

We went to Dad's office for family time.

Iris never knew when Frank would need her or she would have to run an errand for him. The home phone rang at all hours with people calling for his care.

> *Many years later, one of Dad's nurses said to me, "I wasn't around your mom as much, but know her as one of the sweetest and most sincere persons I know. She also had to have a lot of patience, as she never knew whether your dad was coming or going."*

It was an intense life for all participants, only made possible because Frank insisted that they hire a young woman to help Iris with child care and housework. Several women, often recent high school graduates, filled this role during the next eight years. Iris identified with these young girls, for, in them, she saw herself as she was twenty years earlier. Some carried with them memories of working for the Sweaney family for the rest of their lives.

I received a letter from a woman more than fifty years after she'd worked for my family:

> I came to work in the house in the summer of 1957 and stayed until after Christmas. I was 17 when I was with you guys. I knew your dad was a compassionate person because he did not charge my family for medical care, because he felt sorry for me. I can remember them getting bushels of vegetables for payment for doctor services because people did not have the money to pay them. ...
>
> I can remember the stone jar in the shed behind the house which was filled with sauerkraut. I love sauerkraut. So we dipped in it quite often. ...
>
> Your folks gave me a cookie jar which I still have. In it was a $25 check for my Christmas. I can remember your mom saying that would be the biggest cookies that cookie jar would ever have in it. ...
>
> Your mom and I remained friends for the rest of her life. When my second daughter was born in 1963, she gave me a crocheted dress of pink and white. ...
>
> I've been gone from there since 1958, but I have so many memories of that wonderful town ... I have lots of good memories in that house you grew up in.

The nephew of another woman wrote me after his aunt died. He had found a newspaper article with a picture of my mother taken in 1985 among his aunt's belongings. She had stayed with us the summer of 1960. It had been such an important experience for her that she had clipped my mother's picture out of the newspaper a quarter of a century later and stored it with her own important family papers and mementos.

Thirty-One

In the fall of 1955, Frank carefully planned the birth of his third child. By now he knew that Iris would require another caesarian section. He scheduled it for the day after Christmas. December 26 was a Monday, and in Frank's plan, Iris would teach Sunday school the previous day, bear her child on Monday, and be back in action by the next Sunday.

When Baby Sweaney arrived, the town celebrated, and the sign in the drugstore window announced his arrival: Doc has a boy! While the birth did happen on schedule, the rest of the plan fell apart. Lou Ann came home from first grade for Christmas vacation with a case of the measles and immediately gave it to me. Iris brought my baby brother Jim home from the hospital while still weak and sore from surgery. She now faced two sick little girls needing her attention. Needless to say, she did not teach Sunday school on New Year's Day the following week.

Lou Ann and Debby Sweaney, 1955

*As the oldest sibling, Lou Ann did everything first,
including getting the measles!*

Iris was like most American women in the 1950s. She had her babies at the hospital. The tradition of having babies at home with the assistance of midwives or a kindly neighbor woman was now replaced by treating pregnancy as a medical condition and procedure. Babies born in Holt County between 1952 and 1960 were usually delivered by Frank Sweaney at Fairfax Hospital, and there were a lot of them, since the baby boom was going strong.

Along with the rest of America, Holt County's faith in medical professionals grew even more the year Jim Sweaney was born, 1955, as that was the year Jonas Salk's polio vaccine was released. Polio was especially feared because it was so indiscriminant. The dreaded disease had even crippled Franklin Delano Roosevelt. Other vaccines for whooping cough (pertussis) and diphtheria conquered diseases that had previously killed children. All those children that Doc

Sweaney had delivered were brought to his office for polio and DPT shots (a combined vaccine for diphtheria, pertussis, and tetanus). He also treated their parents and grandparents for numerous coughs and routine illnesses that earlier would have been handled by home remedies or, perhaps, may have just cleared up on their own. They liked to come to Doc. Even if his medical treatments did not really cure their ills, he listened to them and made them feel better. Maybe that was part of the problem. They relied on him too much.

His receptionists recorded the names of the patients in his physician's daily record. Beside their names she noted the amount of money they paid for each office visit. Most visits cost two dollars unless medication was distributed; then the charge was three dollars. Many times, the notation N/C indicated that no charge was made. Frank chose not to charge patients for many reasons, but sometimes it was just out of generosity. Iris, the practical one, still worried about bills, and when he thought that he might be being too casual with the collections, he looked sheepishly at his receptionist and said, "Don't tell Iris."

Even with only a small amount collected from each patient, the sheer volume of work meant that more money was being brought in than Frank and Iris had ever seen. Many people depended on that money. In addition to supporting his family, five office staff people had to be paid, and money was also sent to both sets of parents. He was also helping to put his younger sister Goldie through college. Despite all these expenses, enough money was left over so that Iris could buy items that made her feel more secure.

Iris remembered the cold wind that blew through the tarpaper shack when she was a child. She was determined that her children would have an easier life. She bought blankets because she never wanted them to feel cold. She recalled what it was like to go to college with her clothes in boxes, so she bought a set of suitcases for each of her daughters. The smaller vanity case in these sets had a mirror in the lid. Lou Ann's suitcases were light blue, with the initials LAS inscribed on a metal plate in the center of the suitcases. Mine were light green with the letters DLS. Iris also allowed herself to purchase the additional spoons and forks in her silver pattern that she needed to complete her set. Still, her emphasis was on security rather than luxury. She began college savings accounts for each of her children and bought government savings bonds with any extra money. Each bond was registered in her and Frank's name, and then also in the name of one of her children.

Frank did not worry about the future in the same way. He bought things to make their life easier and to add beauty to it. Like most Americans, he bought a new car. He put a lot of mileage on his vehicles, so he got a new one every few years. Soon he moved up to Olds 98s, the top of the Oldsmobile line. His Olds was black, and people in the small community knew it well. When they saw it parked outside a home, they knew someone inside was sick.

Frank wanted to make his wife's life easier and to give her nice things, so he bought her a blue Chevrolet station wagon, new appliances, and for the first time, she had her own washer and drier. He picked out a full-length fake fur coat for her, which she wore proudly. Knowing her love for pretty things, he bought a hand-painted china punchbowl set and an antique chandelier.

In the summer of 1958, Frank came home one afternoon with a home movie camera. These cameras were popular with the baby boom fathers who wanted to capture their children on film. When the cost of the cameras dropped, they became affordable for the average American. Ozzie and Harriet Nelson, whose weekly television show was sponsored by Kodak, explained to viewers how easy it was to make home movies, and then proceeded to show their own purported home movies of their sons David and Ricky Nelson water skiing and engaged in other activities. Obviously, the Nelsons' home movies were much more professional than those turned out by most fathers.

Unbeknownst to Iris, Frank filmed the chaotic scene as she tried to get her family ready for their movie debut. Her maternity clothes were fashionable, but they are not the least bit flattering to a woman who had just turned forty and was seven months pregnant with her fourth child. She tried to comb and part my fine hair, and then turned to arrange Lou Ann's hair. It was difficult to get her three-year-old son, Jim, to stand still long enough to arrange his clothes and hair. The family's black Cocker Spaniel, Midnight, was so excited by the preparations that he added to the chaos by jumping all over everyone. Finally, Iris signaled to Frank that we were ready to be filmed. Frank, the movie director, directed his family to move toward the camera, so we linked arms and walked very stiffly toward him. It was not until a month later, when the film was processed, that Iris realized her preparations had been filmed.

It was typical of her husband to tease her in such a manner, and the film remains as one of the few documents of our family life. Even though Frank does not appear on camera, the short movie tells a great deal about his personality.

In September 1958, Iris delivered her last child. She was in the hospital for a week after another caesarian section. Frank planned to surprise her by having the kitchen in the old house remodeled while she was recuperating. He swore his daughters to secrecy, but was unable to keep the secret himself. From Frank's broad hints, Iris knew all about the surprise before she came home.

Iris named the new baby Carry after her own mother, and very soon after, she bought a set of light blue suitcases with the initials CAS on them.

Thirty-Two

By the end of the 1950s, things started to fall apart. Finn and Carrie McCluey could no longer stay by themselves, so Frank and Iris brought them to Oregon to live. They rented a house for them near Frank's office. It was yet another responsibility for Iris.

It was during this time that the pace of Frank's life caught up with him. For eight years, he had fueled his intense life with caffeine, sugar, and carbohydrates. His lack of sleep, constant work, and poor diet caused his health to deteriorate. He grew obese, probably developed diabetes, and his blood pressure skyrocketed. He simply was not capable of altering the situation, and by then it may have been too late. He kept going, though, and tried to compensate. He had people drive him on house calls so he could catch quick naps between patients, but this was not enough, and his body began to rebel against the abuse. His kidneys and heart started to fail.

As Iris watched her husband's health crisis unfold, she became more and more anxious. She felt powerless and began to have nightmares. One night she woke up from a particularly vivid one. In it, she heard a knock on the door and opened it to find a man she did not know.

"I'm sorry, Mrs. Sweaney," the stranger said, "Doc had an accident."

Iris woke up still shaking and hearing the man's words over and over again. She ran to the phone and called the local sheriff's office to see if they had found his car. There had been no accident.

Sheriff Ramsey's wife said, "The sheriff is not here. He is on house calls with Doc."

His office staff knew that Doc's health was failing. They heard him vomiting in the bathroom. They tried to respond by encouraging patients to respect office hours, but by then it was too late to change their habits and expectations. By June 1960, Frank suspected that he was dying. He took his family for one last trip to see his parents in the Ozarks.

It is the only time I remember our entire family taking a vacation together. My father had taken no time off in the eight years since moving to Oregon. The last night before we came home lives in my memory as an idyllic summer night that only children can experience. I played with my Sweaney cousins, chasing each other in the large yard. Under Grandma Sweaney's direction, we took turns cranking the handle of an old ice cream maker. We hit an old rusty nail with a hammer to create air holes in the metal lids of old glass jars and then filled them with some of the many fireflies that were lighting up the night. We competed to see who could catch the most insects. The trip was over far too soon, as we returned to Northwest Missouri the next day.

As a seven-year-old child, I was not aware that my father was saying goodbye. Before the month of June was over, Iris

Sweaney took her husband to Missouri Methodist Hospital in St. Joseph, the hospital where just ten years earlier he had been a promising resident. My mother was constantly by his side. When he slept, she prayed.

Frank lasted about a month. There was no medical treatment yet for the hypertension that was destroying his vital organs. He died on July 18, 1960, his wife's forty-second birthday. Grief-stricken, Iris left the hospital and returned to Oregon. On her way home, she tried to find the right words to tell her young children that their father was not coming home.

Thirty-Three

Reverend Charles Hagee of the Mound City Christian Church had a difficult assignment on July 20, 1960: He was called to console a grieving community. He looked at the faces of those gathered in the Oregon Christian Church. It was not his home church, but the people came from all over Northwest Missouri. Already, the church was overflowing, and many people were openly crying. It was hot inside the brick building. The funeral parlor fans, with their colored pictures of Jesus stapled to a wooden stick, did little to cool the air. Outside, the Missouri State Highway Patrol was still directing traffic and trying to help people find a parking place.

The soloist rose and sang:

> What a friend we have in Jesus,
> All our sins and griefs to bear!
> What a privilege to carry
> everything to God in prayer!
> Oh, what peace we often forfeit,
> Oh, what needless pain we bear,
> all because we do not carry
> Everything to God in prayer!

Reverend Hagee walked to the pulpit and turned to the Gospel of Matthew. He read out loud, "Come to me, all you who are weary and burdened, and I will give you rest," and then began to speak:

"I am sure everyone here within the sound of my voice, and as far as that is concerned, all of the people in this section of Missouri, have asked the question, 'Why did Dr. Sweaney have to go? He enjoyed life and sought to do for others. He was just at the prime of life; and seemingly at the height of a career of service.' This shows that we are finite. Yes, he was so young in years. Only yesterday, in our little town, a man whose hair was white, and whose shoulders were stooped, stopped me on the street. He said, 'Preacher, will you answer me this question: Why did Dr. Sweaney have to go when he was so needed, and was so helpful? He was at the height of service to his fellow men, and here I am, left no particular good to anybody else or myself?'

"We have placed a measuring stick upon time. We measure it by the calendar, but life is eternal. Dr. Sweaney knew nothing of time as far as days, night, months, or years, but he thought only in terms of service for his fellow men. Wherever there was suffering, and wherever he was called, he was there. Let us remember our Savior was only 33 years of age when He responded to the call of God, and went to the Cross for us. May this be like a spring breeze from a life that was lived unselfishly, and measured in service to his fellow men.

"The practical side of life is more appealing than the eternal side to most of us. God will take care of us if we, His children, do His bidding. We see lives around us lived in such an abundant way. He, like the Savior, came that we might have life more abundantly. His life was free from selfishness and criticism. When I think of him I cannot think of him as being gone. His life shall linger on; his life shall live in the goodness of your life and mine. It shall inspire you to greater and more abundant life and living. It will give you something for which to live, not only for this life, but for the life which is to come.

"May these memories inspire and bless, and may his memory be a blessing to each one of us. May I ask you to live a life of service and sacrifice. May it be an inspiration to all of us to live the abundant life. We who call ourselves Christians have a greater ideal and challenge than he, even though we did not take the oath. It is that we may be able to render unto our fellow men and unto God more service. His life is but gone for the physical; but for the eternal it shall long live in the lives of such a multitude of people.

"Only in the wisdom of God can we explain why we had to give this one up. May we so live that our lives will be a great blessing to those about us, as he did. His life was not measured in years, but in service to all. May God bless and comfort our hearts at this time, and inspire us to serve Him and our fellow men as did Dr. Sweaney."

The people who listened understood his message. They had already written Iris, intertwining her husband's work and God's. Rev. Hagee's words comforted them. But the two women sitting in the front pew, who loved Frank the most, did not hear the words.

Eva Sweaney, Frank's mother, sat weeping inconsolably, unable to hear any words. Her daughter-in-law Iris sat stoic on the pew beside her. She was numb.

Thirty-Four

Ten days later, with the words pouring out of her, Iris sat at a table with a pen and paper and began to write her father's obituary. Finn McCluey had died the previous day, his emphysema choking his breath for the last time. Iris began:

> *Thomas Finley McCluey, Finn to his family and friends, died on July 29 at Fairfax Hospital. Except for the last year of his life, he lived on the land on which he was born.*

The rest of the McCluey family had just gotten settled in their homes in the Ozarks after attending Frank's funeral. They now had to return to North Missouri. Again, they gathered at the Oregon Christian Church. Like mourners at McCluey funerals for over three centuries, they heard the ancient words of the psalmist: "Yeah, though I walk through the Valley of the Shadow of Death, I will fear no evil."

Iris sat through another funeral in which she did not hear the preacher's words. At that moment, the twenty-third psalm did not offer her comfort.

Her mother, Carrie, was beside her. Because of her hearing loss, Carrie's family wasn't sure if she heard the words. No one ever knew Carrie's thoughts or emotions.

Finn McCluey was buried far from McCluey land in the Oregon cemetery. Next to his grave was the mound still covered with fresh dirt where his son-in-law's body lay.

A few weeks later, Iris and her sister Avis cleaned out their parent's rental house together. There was no way that Carrie McCluey could live by herself. She was now an old woman, frail and hard of hearing. Her two youngest daughters assumed the responsibility for her care. Iris was the first to take her turn housing their mother.

Grandma Carrie came to live in our home.

I Come to
the Garden Alone

Thirty-Five

The dew was still on the roses when Iris visited the cemetery on Memorial Day in 1961. Before she left home, she filled old Miracle Whip jars with peonies—flowers for the two graves. She placed the larger bouquet on Frank's gravestone and the smaller one beside her father's grave. In the quietness of the cool morning, she felt her husband's presence and heard his voice. The words of the old hymn played out in her head:

> I come to the garden alone
> While the dew is still on the roses
> And the voice I hear falling on my ear
> The Son of God discloses.
> And He walks with me, and He talks with me,
> And He tells me I am His own;
> And the joy we share as we tarry there,
> None other has ever known.
>
> He speaks, and the sound of His voice,
> Is so sweet the birds hush their singing,
> And the melody that He gave to me
> Within my heart is ringing.
>
> I'd stay in the garden with Him
> Though the night around me be falling,
> But He bids me go; through the voice of woe
> His voice to me is calling.

Both graves had already been prepared for the women who someday would lie beside their husbands. On Frank's stone, her name, Iris McCluey Sweaney, was already carved on the stone, and the name Carrie was etched beside Finn's name. For the fifteen years of her married life, she was my father's helpmate. Each day's schedule revolved around his medical practice. She planned her meals around his needs. She saw her place in the town as Doc Sweaney's wife. At forty-two, she was now defined as his widow.

It had been a difficult year for Iris and her young family. There were constant reminders of Frank. The mail brought notices in his name, and she returned them, marked, *The doctor is deceased*. She tried to fight off the depression and anxiety that came with grief. She was tired and was not sleeping well. She could no longer sleep in the bed that she and Frank had shared, where they had created their four children. There were too many memories. Too often, when she did fall asleep, she had vivid nightmares.

The house was full of emotions, as each person dealt with loss and the changes that had occurred for our family. Carry, her youngest, woke up many nights with her own vivid nightmares. At eight, I developed severe strep infections that no amount of antibiotics could cure. Iris again spent nights beside a bed in a hospital as she watched me fight off the disease. I did not begin to recover until the next year, when I had my tonsils removed. Their first born, Lou Ann, missed her father terribly, and Jim, her only son, would have to grow up without a male role model. Her mother, Carrie, also required her attention. Carrie was not stable on her feet. Iris worried that her mother might fall and did not want to leave her home alone at night. Consequently, Iris's interaction with other adults was curtailed.

Each month that year brought its own special challenge. December was especially difficult. Iris did not cry on December 22; it would have been her sixteenth wedding anniversary. The previous year, Frank played Santa Claus at the VFW's party for the town's children. Iris now had to play that role for her children by herself. February brought its own memories. Frank had always given her a gift on Valentine's Day. Now she treasured the costume jewelry in her blue keepsake box.

She was reminded that her role in town had changed shortly after these holidays. As the doctor's wife, she had been invited to join several of the women's clubs in town. Membership in these clubs denoted social standing. Two society matrons from one of the clubs came to visit her. They asked her if she still wanted to be a member. Perhaps they did not mean to be insensitive, but my mother was offended. Still carrying slights from her high school days, she took it to mean that they no longer welcomed her. She told them, "No, with four small children and an aging mother, I do not have the time for club meetings."

Her childhood left deep scars. She remembered the poverty of the Ozark Mountains and what it was like not to be accepted by the girls in her class. These memories haunted her and seemed to increase with the depression that came with grief. She was quick to take slight and prone to carry grudges. I always thought that my parents complemented each other well. He brought out her sense of humor and made her feel valued. His love encouraged her and gave her confidence. In turn, she grounded him a bit. Now, with him gone, she lost much of this sense of balance.

The anger that comes with grief was also there. She could not let herself aim any of this emotion toward Frank. She, as well as the community that he served, was well on the way of deifying him, of turning him into an iconic figure. How could she be angry at such an unselfish and giving man? Her faith did not allow her to question the Almighty's wisdom or direct her anger toward her God. So she directed this anger toward others.

On that Memorial Day, she looked at her name on the gravestone. She knew she did not have the luxury of sitting in her chair and waiting for the end of her days. It had been ten months since her husband died. Iris pushed down her own grief and came to grips with her most pressing concern. There was little money coming into her house, and she needed to earn a living. Her children and mother depended on her. Iris could have taken a different path; there were men who came sniffing around. When you moved beyond the sadness in her eyes, you could still see an attractive woman; however, remarriage was not the route she chose.

She thought she had just one skill, one gift. She knew how to teach young children. Education had changed since she taught at the Vawter School. By 1961, the State of Missouri required all public school teachers to hold a bachelor's degree. It did not matter that she had previously been employed for six years as a teacher; however, kindergarten was not yet included in the public curriculum. That summer, Iris remodeled the area of our house where her husband had seen patients. With the help of her sister Avis and her brother-in law, she knocked down a wall and created a school room. She opened a home-based kindergarten for the town's children. She was able to work at home and take care of her two younger children who were not yet in school.

A small group of five-year-olds came to our home that year for a half day each morning. Iris's son, Jim, was in that first kindergarten class. He had trouble sharing his mother with his classmates. She devised a method of controlling her class and disciplining misbehavior. A *naughty* chair sat in a corner. More often than not, it was her son who had to sit in that special seat.

Class wasn't just for playtime. Iris taught lessons. The children memorized the alphabet, recognized basic words, and learned how to add and subtract numbers. She read out loud to them books that her students at the old Stone School in South Missouri had enjoyed. Most importantly, they learned how to behave in a classroom. Mrs. Sweaney prepared them for Mrs. Lark's first-grade class.

It was only recently that I realized the influence my mother had on the children of Oregon. I heard a common refrain among people younger than me: "I don't remember your father, but I loved your mother."

One woman, now in her late fifties, wrote me this year. She attended my mother's kindergarten:

> *Mrs. Sweaney's words are stuck in my head forever. One morning last spring, when I awoke, I said to myself, A birdie with a yellow bill hopped upon the window sill, cocked his shining eye and said, 'Ain't you 'shamed, you sleepy-'ead?*

She continued:

> *Your mother must have loved Robert Louis Stevenson. I also remember her reading another of his poems:*

In winter I get up at night
And dress by yellow candle-light.
In summer quite the other way,
I have to go to bed by day.

I have to go to bed and see
The birds still hopping on the tree,
Or hear the grown-up people's feet
Still going past me in the street.

And does it not seem hard to you,
When all the sky is clear and blue,
And I should like so much to play,
To have to go to bed by day?

I closed my eyes. I could see my mother's copy of *A Child's Garden of Verses*, and I heard her voice reciting this poem.

Fifty years after she closed her small kindergarten, one of the small children's chairs from her kindergarten class room is featured in an exhibit at the Holt County Museum and Research Center. It serves as a testament to the impact that she had on the children of the community.

Thirty-Six

My mother loved the classic children's stories, and she read them to me before my father died. She was carrying on the tradition of her mother, Carrie. One of my favorite stories was the *Boxcar Children*.

I read this story to first graders this year. Henry, Jessie, Violet, and Benny Alden set up home in an old boxcar. They are fleeing their grandfather, who they assume is cruel. The two older children take on adult roles and keep Violet and Benny safe. Without any adult supervision, the children make out just fine through their own ingenuity and creativity.

At seven, I loved the idea of sleeping on a bed of pine needles in the old boxcar, keeping the milk cold under a waterfall, and working together to build a dam to create a swimming hole. The story comes to a climax when Violet gets sick and they must recruit adult help in the form of kindly Dr. Moore. The good doctor introduces them to a very nice man who just happens to be their grandfather Alden. The grandfather not only turns out to be kind and loving, but also wealthy.

This children's classic from Gertrude Chandler Warner still entertains. The copyright date is 1942, but the fears of that decade of war and destruction are not to be found. This book is clearly written during the Great Depression, with its message of hard work and self-reliance. As I started to read the next chapter to my first graders, I saw eighteen pairs of eyes eagerly awaiting my words. It was fun to watch these twenty-first century children as they heard the story of the Alden children, written seventy-five years earlier.

One pretty little blonde girl caught my attention as she looked at me with sensitive eyes. She recognized a reality that children usually miss.

Rather sorrowfully, she said, "Their parents died."

"Yes, I know," I said. "Isn't that sad?"

Mom first read the *Boxcar Children* to me the summer after I was in the first grade. The next summer, my father died. In many ways, I also lost my mother that summer. I had been her little girl. In first grade, she fixed my hair, braiding two small strands and fastening the braid with a colorful band. She tied the wide sash of my dress into a bow that stood up almost as if it were starched. As I approached third grade, I watched my mother change. Worries, sorrow, and grief dominated her face. She no longer had time to brush my hair.

Like the boxcar children, there were four Sweaney children, but we didn't share the fun adventures of the Aldens. It is hard to describe how much our life changed with my father's death. Like the children in the story, we began to take on adult roles. Throughout the next years, I cooked many of our family meals. I absorbed my mother's worries about money and was a little embarrassed that we did not have as much disposable income as my peers. The Sweaney children shared another experience with the boxcar children: We were disconnected from our father's family, partly due to distance, but more likely because the Sweaney and McCluey emotional makeup was different and they grieved differently. Sadly, the two families who loved Frank Sweaney could not help each other cope with the incredible loss they both felt.

I took to heart the words of several well-meaning church women who told me that I needed to grow up and help my mother. Mom asked me what I wanted for Christmas that first year after Dad died. I told her I was too old to play with dolls. She bought Carry a wonderful life-like baby doll with sweet rosy cheeks. I held Carry's present much of Christmas Day. The day after Christmas was cold and icy. The roads were not safe. My mother put on her warmest coat and boots and walked five blocks to Scheib's Hardware to buy another doll for me. (This doll now rests on the pillows of the bed in my guest room.)

A year and half later, my mother had a short stay in the hospital. I did not know what was wrong with her, but I knew she was sick. She was only there for about a week, but I assumed that she was dying. This fear felt rational to me; after all, both my father and grandfather died when they went to the hospital. It was the first week of September and school had just started. Lou Ann stayed with her best friend, and Jim and Carry stayed with Aunt Avis. One of those well-meaning church women took me into her home for the week. It was the scariest week of my life.

I am sure that the good woman had no idea the turmoil that I was experiencing. She did not give me any comfort or assurance that my mother would return soon, but Mom came home the next Saturday, and the woman took me to see her. Before we entered our house, the woman with whom I had stayed told me I would be staying with her for a few more days, as my mother needed to rest. Mom was lying on our couch. The moment I saw her, I began crying and hugging her. The woman took hold of me and led me outside. She yelled at me and told me she could just spank me for crying and causing my mother pain. I was a *good* little girl, and no one yelled at me. That episode haunted me for years. I can still remember the fear I felt that week.

In 2013, I returned to the land of my childhood after writing *Unpacking Memories.* I was surprised that so many people younger than me remembered my mother as such a nurturing figure. I had lost that image of her. In my mind, the mother of my childhood was wrapped in depression and grief. I forgot the mother who existed before my father died. As I heard the memories of the children she taught in kindergarten, I remembered the woman who tied my sash into a big bow, brushed and braided my hair, and walked in the snow to buy me a doll. I missed her.

Thirty-Seven

Don Palmer, the superintendent of the Oregon Public School, had a problem. The year 1966 had been a difficult one for him, but it was not over yet. The county had been wracked by a very messy school consolidation fight, and the small town schools of Oregon and Forest City were going to merge the next fall into one school, South Holt. It was hard work to deal with the intensity of people's feelings about their local schools. He was also faced with another emotionally draining situation: The public school was going to offer free kindergarten that fall. He had to deliver the bad news to Mrs. Sweaney. Her home-based kindergarten would be forced to close.

He knew Mrs. Sweaney well, and like most people in Holt County, he felt compassion for our family. Every Sunday, he watched us sit closely together at the Oregon Christian Church. We four kids always were right next to our mother, in the same pew, on the north side of the church. Lou Ann babysat his children. His young son attended Mrs. Sweaney's kindergarten. He knew it would be a hard blow. His hands were tied. Like so many people with a difficult task, he just put it off.

My mother did not officially hear the news first from him; she heard it at Kreek's Grocery Store. A woman came up to her and said, "Iris, I am so sorry to hear that you will have to close your kindergarten." The woman was known more for her gossipy tongue than for her compassion.

The next day, Mr. Palmer called my mother and asked if he could stop by and see her. He delivered the school board's decision to start a public kindergarten. Of course, he could not offer her a job teaching. On paper, she was not qualified. Instead, he offered her a teacher's aide position in the kindergarten classroom. My mother felt she had no choice but to accept. That fall was the beginning of what would turn out to be difficult years for our family.

Iris Sweaney was no longer in charge of her classroom; she was simply there to help the teacher. The South Holt kindergarten went through a series of teachers the next four years. Some of them were young women just out of college, barely twenty-one. Their plan was to teach for a year and then be married. My mother taught them how to be a teacher. One of these women wrote me in 2013:

> *Your mother was my teacher's aide when I taught kindergarten at South Holt 1969-1970. She was a wonderful person and I learned so much from her. She had sooo much patience with the children and guided them without saying a word. I'll never forget her.*

There was a pecking order among school employees, and teacher aides were considered just above the kitchen staff. The teacher aides were expected to always be on the playground during recess. They stood and watched the children play, broke up fights, and wiped tears away from the little faces when someone was physically hurt or teased. One woman told me her memory a couple of years ago:

"I fell on the cement that surrounded the swings. I scraped my knees and legs. The amount of blood made it look more serious than it really was. Your mother picked me up and carried me into the school, where she wiped off the blood and put band-aids on my scrapes."

My mother's actions had obviously made a lasting impression on her. As she told me the story, I could see that she was remembering that long ago day. She repeated herself:

"She was a small woman, and I was almost as big as her. But she just picked me up and carried me."

In winter, playground duty was especially difficult for my mother. Missouri winters are hard. Even when there is no snow or ice, there is the cold, cold wind. I have heard Missouri wind described as "lazy." It never goes around you, but always takes the shortest, easiest path. It just cuts right through you. No matter how much she wrapped herself in a warm coat, boots, scarves, and gloves, she froze on the playground and was miserable. When she came home at night, there were her four children, demanding attention, and bills to pay. And she always had to contend with the loneliness.

Evenings were not easy in our house. Mom was anxious and worried about money. She was never a good housekeeper, and clutter reigned. The old clapboard house needed attention. It had stood for over seventy years, but it now required maintenance, care, and renovation. It was expensive to heat the big old drafty house, and the old furnace did not always work well. It needed replacing, but that would have been costly. It was also legitimate to worry that the house was a fire trap.

My mother looked forward to summer, when she would have a three-month break from school and the weather. She could spend time in her beloved garden.

Thirty-Eight

My mother loved the time in her garden. That quiet time centered her and allowed her to cope with the many pressures of the coming day. She woke up early in the late spring and summer. She put on old clothes and was in her garden before anyone else in the house arose. She loved watching the young plants push their way out of the dark soil to seek the hot Missouri sun. She pulled weeds by hand and pulled off bugs and worms that dared to attack her plants, crushing them under her shoe.

She did not grow flowers. Vegetables grew out of her soil. She was always practical and said, "I do not want to plant anything that I cannot eat." We enjoyed their freshness during the summer. By the end of the growing season, her basement shelf contained mason jars full of green beans and canned tomatoes. Other tomatoes were boiled and then pushed through the fine holes of a colander. My mother added just the right combination of spices to the liquid and made the best tomato juice I have ever tasted. She never measured the spices, but it always turned out the same.

Nothing was to be wasted. Pumpkins were not just for carving, but to be turned into pies. We did create jack-o'-lanterns, but not until a few days before Halloween. If a jack-o'-lantern stood too long, it would spoil and could not be eaten. We also had several apricot trees on our property. My mother would pick up the fruit that fell on the ground, take out her colander, and as she did with the tomatoes and the pumpkins, she used a heavy wooden mallet to push the fruit through its small holes. She turned the heavy pulp into rich, dark marmalade.

I always thought that Mom's apricot marmalade was a unique recipe, one that she had created mixing just the right degree of sugar, spices, and apricot pulp to form the thick jelly. It was at a Pennsylvania farmer's market that I learned about Mom's marmalade. These markets, full of Amish and Pennsylvania Dutch treats, are all over Central Pennsylvania in the spring and summer. At one stand featuring homemade jellies, a pretty dark orange jar labeled Apricot Marmalade caught my eye. It instantly reminded me of my mother, and I bought it.

When I opened the jar the next day and tasted the rich jelly, I was transported back to Mom's kitchen. I could see her pushing the apricots through her colander, the pulp forming in the bowl. The taste of that Pennsylvania Dutch marmalade was just like hers. I remembered my Great-Grandmother Anna Swartz, who migrated from Pennsylvania to the Midwest, bringing Pennsylvania Dutch traditions with her. I understood for the first time that Mom had not just created that wonderful concoction; it had come down to her from women who came before her.

The lessons that my mother learned from these women went beyond recipes. Her mother and grandmother passed on their method of dealing with life's adversities. My mother's survival instincts took her back to the years of the Great Depression. As she faced her own challenges, Iris responded much as she saw her parents respond during her own childhood. She had been raised on the principle of coping with circumstances that are not of your own making. You kept working and prayed. Perhaps the three women all would have said, "What choice do we have?" But many people would have made other choices or would have given up. My mother did not. She somehow found the inner strength to persevere, to get through the darkest days.

I once asked my Aunt Avis' daughter Marilyn about our Grandma Carrie. Her life seemed so sad and difficult to me.

"Do you think Grandma missed drawing?" I asked. "She was so creative. Do you think she was unhappy?"

"I can see why you might ask," Marilyn said, "but I don't think so. After all, she had her garden."

Somehow, in the act of tilling the soil and nurturing the young plants, these women found inner peace. They felt joy in seeing a small seed turn into a healthy plant full of juicy red tomatoes. Gardening is not at all passive. It requires hard work. But regardless of your own efforts, you are still at the mercy of forces outside of your own control. You can follow all the rules, but rain may not come and pests may attack your plants. For these women, this truth governed not only gardening but their very existence.

Iris McCluey Sweaney was different, though. Unlike her mother, she eventually moved beyond just accepting life as it was. Ten years after my father died, she charted a new course for herself. It required courage. It was risky. In doing so, she not only found talents that she did not know she possessed, but also a great deal of personal fulfillment.

Thirty-Nine

It was January 1970, the start of a new decade. I was a senior in high school and would soon leave Oregon, Missouri. I did not know then that my life would take me far from my small town roots. My mother was also moving on, although not in terms of her locality. She would stay in Oregon for the rest of her life, but her changes were just as significant as mine, for during this decade, she moved away from living in my father's shadow.

If the future paths of our lives were not clear that spring, we were not alone. The traditional rules of society that governed the roles of women were breaking apart at their seams. Grandma Carrie had joined the WCTU during those early years of the twentieth century and saw the temperance movement morph into the suffrage movement. The passion of those women secured the right to vote for Carrie's daughters. Fifty years later, women's rights were again the topic of conversations. The emerging feminist movement was forging monumental changes for American women. I would have a different life than my mother's because of these changes.

Iris McCluey Sweaney never identified herself as any kind of an activist, but she wanted a happy and prosperous life for all her children. It was her life mission to see that her children went to college. It was especially important to her to prepare her daughters for the future. She never actually uttered the words, *"Your husband might die,"* but that sentiment lived in our house. As I prepared to leave home, it was not a future husband's death that worried me; I was worried about my mother's health. She no longer could stand the playground duty and knew she needed to leave her school job.

The Iris Sweaney family

This picture was taken shortly before Lou Ann left for college in 1967. Lou Ann and I are in the back row; Carry, Iris, and Jim are in the front row.

I did not understand that at fifty-two her body was changing. Hormonal fluctuations were affecting her not only physically but emotionally. It was a subject that was not yet talked about in polite society. Daytime talk shows were not discussing the physical changes that happen to women during the course of their lives. Female comediennes did not make jokes about hot flashes. As always, when my mother was not well, I was scared. She was scared also, and her anxiety permeated our house. With Grandma Carrie's passing a few years earlier, she no longer had the responsibility of caring for an aging parent. But in the fall, her two oldest daughters would be in college, her son was just beginning high school, and her youngest was in junior high.

She did not yet know the truth that many women discover. When a woman is in her fifties, it can be an empowering decade for many, and stories abound about women taking their lives in new directions during those years. In her twenties, Iris McCluey emerged from her parents' home, became a teacher, fell in love, and was married. In her thirties, Mrs. Frank Sweaney had babies and supported her husband. In her forties, Iris Sweaney survived. Now, in her fifties, her life took a new direction. In the twenty-first century, we would say that she found her voice.

For my mother, the next stage in her life started when a former school teacher knocked on our door. By 1970, Lois Hood was retired from teaching. She filled her time by dabbling in local politics and was a Republican committeewoman. It was in that capacity that she came to see my mother that spring. She wanted my mother to run for a county office, specifically that of tax collector. Iris McCluey Sweaney would have to run against the current officeholder, a man by the name of Don Beesley.

Don Beesley had deep roots in Holt County. He was well known as the leader of a very popular musical group, Don Beesley & the Country Gentlemen. Previously, he served three consecutive terms as the Holt County assessor and was now in his first term as the collector. It was a step up to be the collector from the assessor's office. The tax collector was the most lucrative of the county offices, since the officeholder received a portion of the tax collected. It would be a competitive election. Iris Sweaney took a deep breath. It took courage, but she decided to do it. So in the spring of 1970, she gathered the necessary signatures on the petition and threw her hat in the ring. Her name was to appear on the Republican ballot in the primary to be held in August.

On April 11, 1970, shortly after my mother made this major decision, Don Beesley had a heart attack and died. My mother felt more than a twinge of guilt. Did her decision contribute to his heart attack? The filing deadline was extended. His widow filed for his seat. My mother felt compassion for any recent widow, but there was no backing down. Before the deadline was again closed, two men joined the two widows on the ballot for the Holt County Office of Collector of Revenue.

The situation became even more problematic. Democrat Warren Hearnes was the sitting governor of Missouri. He had the obligation to name a successor to fill Don's unexpired term. He looked for a Democrat to name as collector, and chose a generally well-liked insurance salesman from Mound City, Dean Johnson. Even if my mother made it through the primary, she would face opposition from a man who held the office, but she had made a commitment, and Iris Sweaney never walked away from a commitment. She ordered business cards and promotional emery boards with the words Vote for Iris Sweaney, Republican Candidate for Holt County Collector of Revenue printed on them.

That summer, Monday through Saturday, she awoke early and spent an hour in her garden, pulling up weeds, and checking on each plant, and then she washed up and changed into a dress and stockings. She packed a lunch and started out in her car. She first drove north into the area where farmers tilled the soil in the rich Missouri River bottoms. She drove down the old dirt roads, stopping at the farmhouses along the way. The farm women invited her in for a cup of coffee, and together they shared memories of her husband. They all had a story about Doc Sweaney to tell. Iris would hand out an emery board after each visit, get back in her car, and drive to the next house. Later in the summer, she walked around Oregon, Mound City, and Forest City, where the houses sat closer together. She again handed out her emery boards and talked about her late husband and her children.

Iris encountered some scary moments during her visits. A few of the residents did not trust any politician and would close the door quickly. At one old farmhouse, a big dog came out to meet her. He looked friendly enough until he bared his teeth and lunged at her. She ran back to her car, but he grabbed her coat with his big teeth before she could opened the door and get behind the wheel to safety. She was lucky that morning had been cold, because she had put on a lightweight coat. It was pretty well torn, but the animal had not connected with her flesh.

Once a month that summer, she went to the local Republican club dinner meetings. I loved going to those meetings with her. Republican politicians from across the state came to Holt County to campaign for office. Christopher (Kit) Bond, who was running for Missouri State Auditor, was one such speaker. Everyone knew that the auditor's job was always a stepping stone to higher office. (He later served as a United States Senator.) He brought his political operative with him. It was the first time I heard a major political candidate talk, and I was fascinated with his polished stump speech. I watched his campaign professional gauge the crowd and motion him that it was time to wrap up his talk. I decided that in the fall, I would combine my history studies with classes in political science.

As the August 4 primary election approached, a group of Mom's friends took out a large ad in the July 23 edition of the weekly *Holt County Sentinel*. In big letters, they called on the people of Holt County to VOTE FOR IRIS SWEANEY. In the unlikely case that someone in the county had forgotten about her husband's care for them, her friends reminded the voters:

Political advertisement in the *Holt County Sentinel*

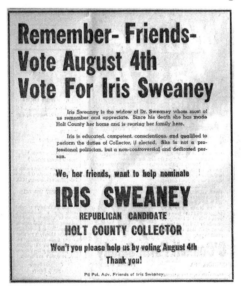

On the first Tuesday in August, the voters of Holt County went to the polls to participate in the American democratic process. The Republican contest for collector of revenue was the race to watch. It was the most contested race in the county, with four Republicans on the ballot. The polling places were set up in grain elevators and public buildings. People accepted their paper ballot from the poll worker and indicated their choice by checking the box beside the name with a pen. Then they dropped the ballot in a locked box.

Jim, Carry, and I dressed in our Sunday best to accompany Mom to the Holt County Courthouse to watch the election returns that night. We sat beside her on a bench in the courtroom. There were no fancy television screens and maps, just a blackboard set up by the witness chair. Written across the top were the fifteen voting precincts in Holt County. Down the side were the names and contests that had appeared on the ballot. As the votes were tallied in each precinct, the counters called the county clerk's office. One by one, the precincts reported their totals. Alvin Mullins, the acting county clerk, brought the results into the courtroom and posted the results for each race and precinct with a piece of chalk.

My excitement grew as he recorded each result. Mom lost by a small margin in a few of the precincts in the northern part of the county. I squeezed her shoulder when the results from the two precincts in Oregon were written on the board. She had overwhelmingly carried them. It was clear that when she got seventy-two votes in Nodaway Township, the night was going in her favor. When the final results were tallied, Iris Sweaney received more votes than the three other Republican candidates combined.

I left for Drake University in Des Moines, Iowa, a few weeks later. I followed the political campaigns that fall closely. Holt County was traditionally a Republican stronghold, but my mother faced general election opposition from the appointed collector, Dean Johnson. She continued campaigning by knocking on doors and handing out her emery boards. She was "on the stump" at the Holt County Fall Festival that September and could be seen at most other events in the county that fall.

It was the first mid-term election after President Nixon's 1968 victory. I watched the results on the television. The November 10, 1970, election did not follow the trend of recent mid-term elections, where the party in the White House loses seats in Congress. Instead, the GOP picked up three seats in the Senate. The Des Moines television stations did not follow the election that personally mattered to me. The Holt County Missouri race for the collector of revenue was not on their radar.

I nervously awaited my mother's call that night, but there was no need for me to be anxious. The final results were Iris M. Sweaney, 1,628, to Dean Johnson, 1,125. Iris Sweaney was to be the next collector of revenue for Holt County. My mother had redefined herself.

Forty

Iris Sweaney was in a new world. She needed help and she turned to Jim Fitzgerald. Jim had always been there to support her family. He had taken the boat to St. Joseph in 1952 to recruit her husband to come to Oregon. He was a retired collector of revenue and became my mother's deputy. He taught her the tricks of the trade. She was a good student.

Iris Sweaney, Collector

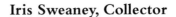

A Bale of Mail

Iris began her new position as collector of revenue. She was now the "boss" and was responsible for collecting more than $1.2 million in taxes. In the above photo from the Holt County Sentinel, she is pictured with her deputies Wilma Sommer and Jim Fitzgerald.

Iris Sweaney proved to be an able administrator. She organized her office well. Like her mother who once created lists of words from newspapers to study, Iris created lists to help guide her. She enjoyed reconciling the county's books. The office workload ran on a cycle. Tax bills came out in the fall and were due by January 1. There was no Christmas vacation for the collector's office. The week between the holidays was busy. The farmers paid for the blessing of fertile land with large tax payments. During the week between Christmas and New Year's Day, the hallway outside the collector's office was crowded with farmers who did not want to fork over the money for their taxes one moment sooner than necessary.

Unlike the twenty-first century, banks were not automated. Numbers were not assigned to accounts and many of the farmers did not carry checkbooks with them. My mother kept a stack of counter checkbooks, one for each bank in the county. A farmer identified the bank that held his money, and my mother or one of her office staff handed him a blank check. He wrote the amount needed to cover his tax bill on the line and signed his name. His signature was the only identification needed for the bank to process the check.

Iris took a coffee break in the middle of the morning each day. She joined the other courthouse workers who gathered in the recorder of deeds office to gossip and relax. Unlike her recent school experience, her position as an elected official ensured that she was given respect. No longer was she on the bottom rung of this social structure. She had earned the recognition herself and it felt good. She connected with other elected officials across Missouri and learned *best practices* from them. During one summer, she traveled to Jefferson City to attend a meeting of the collectors of revenues from across the State. My younger sister, Carry, helped her with her makeup, and she brought along some new clothes. Several of the male collectors made a point of meeting her and giving her guidance.

The new position offered her financial stability, which lessened her anxiety about money. As her old house continued to deteriorate, one of her supportive friends and former ministers, Merrill Ferguson, offered to dismantle it for the lumber. In 1973, my mother made the decision to tear down the house where she had spent her life as a doctor's wife. To me, this decision was her final step in leaving my father's shadow.

I came home the summer after my junior year in college to help with the process of moving out of the big old house. It was hard work to sort through everything we had accumulated over the twenty-one years we had lived in the house, including mementoes of my father's life to pack. In a drawer, I found newspapers in Spanish from Panama announcing the end of World War II and many postcard pictures of the canal. Love letters written during the war were carefully packed along with the other treasures of my parents' life together, as well as records from my father's medical practice, still in file folders. We moved everything into an empty house across the street, where we made a temporary home.

I watched the progress each day as the house of my childhood came apart. Old timers stopped by to watch and shared stories of coming to the house in the middle of the night to fetch Doc Sweaney for some emergency. In the way of a small town, some criticized my mother for her decision to tear down a house that had stood on the lot for three quarters of a century.

It was a bittersweet summer for me. As the boards from my childhood home were pulled apart each day, I felt a deep sadness. The modular house that my mother placed on the lot was never my home. The old house did not completely disappear. It lives in my memories. When I dream of my childhood, I am always in the big white clapboard house that came down piece by piece during the summer I was twenty-one.

The summer of 1973 was the last time I lived in Missouri. Each day I took a break in the afternoon to watch the Watergate hearings on television. A special Senate committee co-chaired by Senators Sam Ervin and Howard Baker investigated the scandal in front of live television cameras. Baker's famous phrase, "What did the President know and when did he know it?" echoed in my Midwestern living room. The parade of witnesses fascinated me, and I gasped with the rest of America when I heard that President Nixon secretly taped his conversations in the Oval Office.

I did not know then that the Watergate scandal would touch me personally.

Forty-One

I flew to Washington, D.C., for the first time in January of 1974. The cab from Washington National Airport took me over Memorial Bridge into the city. The Lincoln Memorial was in front of me. Looking behind me, I saw the eternal flame that marked President Kennedy's grave. I pinched myself. I could not believe I was here.

I came to Washington that winter to spend the final semester of my senior year at the Washington Semester Program at American University. Drake University was among the other schools in the country that sent students to A.U. in Northwest D.C. to give students a firsthand experience with the American political system. We were to write an independent thesis about a current topic and work as an intern in a government office. Jerry Litton, the congressman from Northwest Missouri, gave me the opportunity to work on Capitol Hill.

The name Jerry Litton meant something in Holt County. Although only in his second term in Congress, Litton was a rising star in Democrat circles. His television show *Dialogue with Litton* was broadcast statewide. Among the guests were Jimmy Carter, Secretary of Agriculture Earl Butz, and Tip O'Neill. He added diversity by featuring a conversation with Congresswoman Shirley Chisholm, the first black woman elected to the U.S. Congress. In Republican Holt County, my mother was not alone in proclaiming, "Jerry Litton is a good

Democrat!" Green bumper stickers were already circulating across Missouri with the slogan "Litton for President."

Litton was charismatic and funny. I was star-struck when he invited me to dine with him in the members-only dining room. He pointed out congressmen to me, and I recognized faces from the news. I answered phones in his office that spring, and when a bothersome constituent demanded to speak to him, Litton said, "Tell her that I am on the floor. I don't know what floor I will be on, but I know that I will be on some floor."

The Watergate scandal was the only thing that was discussed among the Washington semester students. Special Prosecutor Jaworski and his investigators were demanding access not only to the Oval Office tapes, but to presidential papers. President Nixon and his lawyers were claiming executive privilege. Nixon, like presidents before him, considered his files and papers to be his personal property. It did not make a lot of sense to me that papers that had been prepared by people who received a government paycheck and were typed by government secretaries should be considered the president's private property; however, that was the tradition.

I chose to examine the presidential library system for my thesis topic. It was timely, since the ownership of presidential papers was being questioned in the courts. Franklin Delano Roosevelt had created the system by making a *gift* of his papers to the American people, and then having his friends donate money to build a library in which to house them. The building was then given back to the government to maintain. Every subsequent president followed this tradition. Richard Nixon cared deeply about his legacy and dreamed about his beautiful library in San Clemente. He was already soliciting money for the building from his friends.

As my college graduation approached, I realized that I needed to think about getting a paying job. I interviewed people in the National Archives' Office of Presidential Libraries and Museums for background information for my paper and learned that internships were available. My thesis was a very forgettable paper and would not have impressed anyone, but I was able to turn the fact that I had written it into my first job. I was hired as an intern in the planning office for Richard Nixon's presidential library. The office was located in the Old Executive Office Building (now known as the Eisenhower Executive Office Building), part of the White House complex. As an intern working in the complex, I was included in the programs developed for White House interns.

In June of 1974, I reported to work. My job was to identify people in photographs with the president. I compared the faces in the photos to participants at meetings listed in the presidential diary. I prepared catalogue entries for each photograph to be used as a reference tool for future historians. I was told a story that there was a picture of President Coolidge with a group of people behind him. One of the people in the background was labeled "unidentified." It turned out to be Harry Truman. I was supposed to keep that sort of thing from happening in the future. It was a fun job, and my manager wanted me to stay on after my internship ended. I was "unofficially" told that I would go with the staff to California at the end of the administration.

For a small town girl from Oregon, Missouri, it was a heady experience. As one of only thirty or so White House interns, I had some unique opportunities. I received a special tour of the Oval Office and was invited to a private reception in the family quarters of the White House given by Julie Nixon Eisenhower. Pam Powell, June Allyson and Dick Powell's daughter, was in charge of the interns. Powell and Allyson were popular movie stars in the forties, and favorites of my mother's. Their names meant as much to her as many of the Washington players that I saw in the elevators.

As the summer continued, the Old Executive Office Building began to feel like a bunker. It was clear that the tide was turning against the President, and his administration could not continue. On Wednesday, August 7, the interns met with Vice President Ford. He was probably in a holding pattern and was able to fit us into his schedule. We each had our individual picture taken with him. The next day, President Nixon resigned and Ford became the first "unelected" president to take the office, as the elected vice president, Spiro Agnew, had been forced to resign. In the intensity of the next few days, those pictures were lost.

I was in the East Room of the White House when President Nixon gave his tearful parting speech to his staff. I moved with the crowd to the window of the Blue Room and watched President and Mrs. Ford accompany the former President and Mrs. Nixon to the waiting helicopter. Nixon's presidential library was on hold as lawyers fought over control of his papers. My promised job was not going to materialize. My boss pulled some strings and found me a position in the White House Office of Records Management.

I was a civil servant on the White House staff. I processed presidential correspondence and White House staff papers, preserving them under strict guidelines for future historians. I worked there through the Ford Administration and into the first years of Jimmy Carter's presidency. I sent my mother artifacts that I knew would mean something to her. I attended the formal arrival ceremony when President Ford greeted Emperor and Empress Hirohito of Japan for their official state visit in 1975. I sent my mother the program from the ceremony. As someone who was touched by World War II, she enjoyed my observation that the empress still walked two steps behind her husband.

In February of 1975, my mother was not feeling well. Her illness was not serious enough for me to fly home, but I wanted to do something special for her. I talked to a friend who wrote letters for the President. She wrote a beautiful note in Ford's name and it was typed on the special stationary reserved just for presidential letters. The president's signature was written with a felt tip pen.

Letter from President Gerald Ford

THE WHITE HOUSE
WASHINGTON

February 20, 1975

Dear Mrs. Sweaney:

Mrs. Ford and I were saddened to learn that you have not been feeling well and we hope this note will find you resting comfortably.

We know the love and encouragement you are receiving from your family and friends must be a great help to you, and we join with them in sending you our best wishes. We hope that you will soon be well again.

Sincerely,

Gerald R. Ford

Mrs. Iris M. Sweaney
Route 1, Box 154
Oregon, Missouri 64473

I knew that the letter had never really been on the president's desk and that the signature had been formed by a machine programmed to move a pen to recreate his strokes, but my mother did not know the process that went into creating presidential letters. She treasured it.

I continued to follow Missouri politics during those years. In 1976, Democratic Senator Stuart Symington retired after a long and distinguished career in the Senate. Jerry Litton had been waiting for this opportunity. He joined a crowded Democratic primary field that included Litton, Symington's son James, former Governor Warren Hearnes, and four lesser known politicians. Litton was clearly pitted against the Missouri Democrat establishment. This election was a necessary stepping stone for the thirty-nine-year-old congressman. Everyone in Northwest Missouri knew Jerry Litton was destined to sit in the Oval Office.

Litton was greeted with cheers in his home town of Chillicothe, Missouri, when the election results were announced. He was the clear winner and would face Republican Jack Danforth in the fall. The congressman, his pretty wife, and his two beautiful small children were photographed all smiles as they boarded a plane to fly to a victory celebration in Kansas City. The next morning, this picture appeared in papers across the country. Printed beside it was an image of wreckage strewn across a runway. It was impossible for the people of Northwest Missouri to grasp the tragic reality. Jerry Litton's plane crashed on takeoff, and everyone on board was killed. The St. Joseph newspaper ran a cover story: "What might have been ..." I called my mother and we both cried.

I worked on my master's degree at night while employed at the White house. I left my job in 1978 after receiving this degree to work for a Washington software development firm. I followed the Washington pattern of moving between contracting firms and government jobs during the next three decades. I fell in love with Jim, got married, bought a home in the suburbs, and stayed for thirty years.

In going through my mother's papers in 2016, I found a collection of memorabilia. Mom's letter from President Ford and the White House arrival program for the Emperor of Japan were among them. She had also saved the special edition of the *St. Joseph News Press* following Jerry Litton's death. I looked at the artifacts and was lost in memories of a small town girl who went to the big city. These memories are not all fun; pain was associated with that time in my life.

Washington, D.C., can be a hard place for smart young women. I was not prepared for the sexism of political Washington and the violence of a big city.

I read the newspaper account from August 3, 1976, that told of Litton's life, death, and the dreams shared for his future by all who knew him. I thought of the man who was going to be president. It was such a sad ending for a life that held such promise.

I put the material aside and stared off into space. I remembered the young girl, just becoming a woman, who flew to Washington, D.C., with such excitement in January of 1974. I smiled when I thought of her. Was I ever really that young and naïve?

Forty-Two

Iris Sweaney served twelve years as Holt County collector. She faced the voters two more times. She had little competition and none of these races were close. Something happened in these subsequent elections. The voters elected Iris Sweaney, not Doc Sweaney's widow, to the position.

Iris Sweaney receives commendation

Iris Sweaney retired with the appreciation of the community she served. Iris is shown in above photo printed in the Tines Observer receiving as a commendation from Bette Williams.

She retired in 1982. By then, her four children had graduated from college. Iris used her time to relax and read books. She kept a list of each book she read, the name of the author, and the date she finished it. It was something her mother would have done. In the summer months, she worked in her garden. When we came home on a visit, we filled our suitcases with mason jars of her tomato juice and marmalade. The neighborhood children had a place in her life. They visited her when she was in her garden, and she would answer their endless stream of questions. Some of the young mothers appreciated the time that Iris gave their children, but others took her for granted. She wrote to me after she retired about the young family who lived across the street:

> *They moved last week and I am not sorry. I was out on the ladder picking apricots, and she went out to her car to go someplace and called her five-year-old girl to come. I heard the girl say, "Mom, can I stay with Iris?" but didn't pay any attention. I heard something and looked down and there was Jennifer. I had her for two hours and didn't even know the woman. When she came home, Jennifer went running home and the woman didn't even thank me.*

My siblings and I were settling into our adult lives by now. My mother breathed a sigh of relief when I married in 1986. My brother, Jim, shortly thereafter received a promotion into the managerial ranks of his company and was relocated to Wichita, Kansas. He still spent many weekends with Mom, but he was also becoming an adult. She still worried about us, as mothers always do, but she was able to let us go. Our mistakes would be our own.

Like so many of her generation, the years of the Great Depression were always with her. In July of 1988, she wrote me:

It is 8:30 and I just got in from my garden. It has been 54 years since the drought of 1934, and that is what this year is likened to, but in some ways, I think this year is worse. 1934 was the start of three of the driest years in American history and we do wonder if that part of history will repeat itself. We, in the United States, have so taken our blessings of rich land and plenty of water for granted. We lived in Southwest Missouri and there were no rivers or streams to supply water, and we do have water here in Northwest Missouri, and those farmers who have irrigation systems will be in pretty good shape with higher prices for what they raise.

In February of 1989, she reconnected with her cousin John, the youngest son of Finn's sister. They began to correspond. She had not heard from him since her mother died. He saved these letters, and his daughter sent them to me in 2016.

That April, my mother decided to visit her daughters and see their homes. We lived on both coasts; Lou Ann and Carry in Northern California and I in the Washington, D.C., area. She bought a new suitcase with wheels on it to make it easy to carry her belongings. It was a far cry from the box that she had used to pack her clothes when she went to summer school at Southwest Baptist College. She did not want to be perceived as playing favorites with her children, so she planned her trip carefully. Her itinerary called for her to spend exactly a week and a half—10 days—in each of our homes. She flew from Kansas City to San Francisco, and then she flew from there to Washington to spend time with me.

Each of us did something special with her. Lou Ann took her to Hearst Castle in San Simeon, William Randolph Hearst's famous estate; Carry took her shopping for new clothes; and when she came to see me in D.C., we visited Pennsylvania to see the Amish country. She was fascinated with these people who livid simply, dressed plainly, and refused to adopt modern technology.

She wrote her cousin John when she returned on May 11:

> *Your letter was here when I got back from my long trip. It was the best trip I have ever taken and the longest. My three girls and their families were all fine.*

She wrote with a sense of pride of each of our lives. In between the lines was an unwritten message: Her life mission was successful. Her family was thriving.

She planned another trip to go back home to Southwest Missouri to see McCluey land one more time. The old tarpaper shack was no longer there, but the tree planted by Robert McCluey for Sarah, the grandmother she never knew, was still guarding the land. She might even be able to pick a few blackberries and see wildflowers again. She planned her trip to coincide with her seventy-first birthday in July. Since her forty-second birthday, she awoke every July 18 thinking *This is the day that Frank died.* Now she was able to look forward to that day as the day that she was born.

It just so happened that at the same time, her high school classmates were getting together to celebrate their fiftieth high school reunion. She wanted to go to this celebration, as all the pain of not fitting into the popular clique at school was far in the past. She remembered the good times. For the next month, she worked on her itinerary. She wrote her classmate who was planning the reunion that she was coming. All the details were in place. It was a pilgrimage that she needed to take.

On June 6, 1989, she wrote to her cousin John. Her letter was full of plans for her trip and news of her garden:

> *I have a big garden and it keeps me busy. I really didn't mean to plant a garden this year, but I did hire a man to plow it last fall, and while I was visiting the kids this spring, one of my friends came over and harrowed it, and just before I came home, another friend came over and tilled it for me. The soil really works nice and things look pretty good, but it is too much work for me. I will be 71 the 18th day of July.*

The trip back to the land of her childhood was not to be. She was in her garden when she felt the pain in her chest. Her four children arrived from homes far away to be with her. She lived a week. The massive attack tore a hole in her heart. Doctors tried to repair it with surgery, but it tore again. We were by her bedside when they took her into the operating room for a final attempt to repair the tear. She did not survive the second surgery. It was July 6, 1989, twelve days before Iris McCluey Sweaney would have turned seventy-one.

She left us the exact details of what she wanted for her funeral and had already paid the funeral home bill. We followed her instructions to the tee. The church was crowded as one of Oregon's leading soloists sang "I Come to the Garden Alone." We ordered Calla lilies for her casket—one of her favorite flowers—and we had a few irises tucked into the arrangement.

Lou Ann, Jim, Carry, and I watched as her casket was lowered into the ground. She was placed beside my father. Her gravestone was waiting for her. It had been twenty-nine years since her name had been etched on it.

Epilogue

July 8, 2017
Carlisle, Pennsylvania

Today is my birthday. It seems appropriate that I wrote the last line of my mother's story the week I turned sixty-five. In doing so, I finished the journey that began when I opened Grandma Carrie's old suitcase five years ago. I traveled through time and found a story that crossed three centuries. I returned to the world of Anna, Carrie, and Iris. Often, I felt tears on my face as I wrote.

I was beside Anna at little Lester's grave and felt Carrie's deep pain as two-day-old Winnifred June was placed in the ground with only a piece of wood marking the site. I saw Carrie's hand as she drew pretty pictures on that trip from Iowa to South Missouri when she was ten. I watched Iris go to the mailbox to see if a letter was there, open it carefully, read it several times, and return it to the envelope with the military censor stamp prominently displayed. I waited with her for Frank's call, telling her that he was safely home from Panama. Again, I was a little eight-year-old girl trying to understand my father's death. I wiped the tears away, but I cannot rewrite the stories. If I did, I would change my own story.

There must be something about this milestone year that makes one remember. *Little House in the Big Woods*, the first of Laura Ingalls Wilder's books, was published the year she turned sixty-five. Laura later said that she wrote because she wanted her parents to be remembered, so she would not lose Pa's stories. I share her feelings. I do not want Anna, Carrie, and Iris to be forgotten. I want to remember them not as some sort of prototypical characters in a novel, but as real people who once lived, loved, and grieved.

My mother was also contemplative the night she turned sixty-five. After my father died, her birthday during my growing-up years was always painful. Like her, I found it difficult to think of it as anything but the day my father died. But as she sat outside on a hot summer night twenty-three years after Frank Sweaney left this earth, her first thought was not of the pain of his death. Instead, she wrote:

July 18, 1983

Things I am thankful for on my 65th birthday.

For telephone calls from Lou Ann and Tory, Hannah, and Joshua [and] from Oona at their mother's house. From Debby, Gwen, and Maxine Edwards (who never forgets). For a bountiful garden and the good health to work in it. For the Beautiful card and call from Avis. For a cool evening to sit in the yard with a beautiful half-moon over the pine tree. For the absence of mosquitoes even after such a wet spring and early summer. For more fireflies than I have seen for years.

For beautiful memories of Frank who has been gone twenty-three years today. So much of his strength of will has "rubbed off" on me and making it possible for me to face the many problems of these years of carrying on alone. For the twelve years' work at the Court House which not only provided financial security but was a great learning experience for me. For a great family—I wish for them each a long and successful life. Most of all for a loving God who has made all this possible.

I hope that my mother can see the life that her children live. We make our homes far away from the land where we grew up, where our father practiced medicine, and where our mother served as an elected official. Carry and Lou Ann live in California, and Jim and I are on the East Coast.

Over the years, we have all weathered some ups and downs, had some health scares, and made our own mistakes. None of us became a *Second Galileo*, as the little boy listening to Frank and Iris on that school bus in 1938 predicted. If that was our potential, we fell short. But we are all blessed by being loved by supportive spouses. For the most part, I think my mother would approve of us.

Lou Ann's daughter Tory grew up in the San Francisco Bay area. She spent childhood summer vacations at her grandmother's house in the small Missouri town not far from the wide, muddy Missouri River where her mother was raised. She visited Sweaney cousins in the Ozarks. I am sure that on at least one warm summer night while in Missouri, she too caught fireflies and put them in a glass jar after making air holes in its lid with a nail.

Tory lives in London now. Those Midwestern memories are little more than vague dreams to her. Her daughters speak English with a British accent. A Missouri twang would sound foreign to their ears. Perhaps one day her daughters will see the tall corn climbing to the sky in the Missouri River bottoms or pick wildflowers in a hollow in the Ozark foothills. And in doing so, they will see where a chapter of their own story, their song, began.

Author's Notes

The descendants of Sarah and Robert McCluey and George and Anna Swartz are scattered over the world. Some still live in Missouri, not too far from McCluey land, but others can be found in Pennsylvania, Kansas, California, North Carolina, and Wyoming. When we left Missouri, we took with us not only memories, but family treasures as well. In each of our homes, the faces of our common ancestors look out from picture frames, and you can see heirlooms that once found a home in Missouri. Few, if any, of these items have monetary worth, but they hold great sentimental value. Other treasures are hidden away, buried at the bottom of cedar chests and in boxes in closets.

When you walk into my sister Lou Ann's house in Marin County, California, the first thing that catches your eye is a beautiful hand-painted punch bowl set. I see it and I am no longer in California, but in the white clapboard house of our childhood. The gift from my father to my mother was the most prized possession in our home. Lou Ann has assured me that the customized wooden cabinet that houses it is earthquake proof. I hope that she is right and that our generation is better able to protect ourselves from the forces of nature than our ancestors were able to do.

In her closet is a box that contains my parents' letters, written to each other in 1944 and 1945. Carry and I spent a weekend carefully copying those letters two years ago so that each of us could have a complete set. We took my father's letters out of his military airmail envelope, carefully unfolded each one, and replaced it just as our mother had done seventy years ago. We do not have a complete set of my mother's letters to our father, but we copied the fifty or so letters from her that were saved. By the time we had finished this project, we had used over two reams of paper. I also found my mother's contracts outlining the terms of her employment in the Dade and Boone County schools in the box.

Carry had my mother's high school graduation diploma and the transcripts from both our father and grandfather's funeral services in a box in her home in San Jose. She also sent me copies of the deed showing the location of George Washington Swartz's property in Iowa. From North Carolina, my brother Jim sent me my father's discharge papers from World War II and the deed to his office building that sat on the courthouse square. Jim has by his fireplace the andirons that our Great-Grandfather Robert McCluey made.

A year ago, I spent a weekend with my cousin Marilyn, the oldest child of Avis McCluey Bullock. She now lives in Kansas. We went through her mother's chest and found items saved by Grandma Carrie, including letters written by my mother as a newlywed from that basement in the boy's boarding house and other letters written home to Missouri from Memphis. Grandma Carrie also saved my father's graduation program from medical school. My cousin David joined us for dinner that night. He has become the keeper of Grandma Carrie's original drawings, created sometime before she was married in 1911. He loaned them to me.

Sheila McCoy Duffy and her siblings live in Wyoming. They are also the great-grandchildren of Anna and George Swartz. Sheila's grandmother was my Grandma Carrie's sister Elba. Sheila and I compared notes about family lore. She too knew the story about our great-grandfather trading his Iowa land for rocky soil in Southwest Missouri. She sent me the location of little Lester's grave in Iowa and a picture I had never seen of my grandmother as a young woman, with the words *Aunt Carrie Swartz* written on the back of it. Sheila is a retired art teacher, and several of her siblings also draw. It seems so unfair to me that Sheila inherited the Swartz artistic genes and I got the hard of hearing genes.

Anita Coiner Southoff still lives in Southwest Missouri. She is also the great-granddaughter of Sarah and Robert McCluey, being the granddaughter of Finn's only sister. She sent me a copy of Robert and Sarah's 1871 marriage certificate. She also sent me the letters my mother wrote her father the summer my mother died. Anita wrote, *My parent's saved everything.* I understand Anita's words. It was a family trait. In my own closet, I have rather uninteresting commercial tourist pictures from Panama bought in 1945. I also have a picture of a young man in an army uniform. He has a cocky grin and his hat is a little askew. On the back, his name, *Johnny*, was written in pencil. I shudder when I see his face. I agree with my Aunt Avis: We are all blessed that my mother did not marry this man.

My mother's sister Avis did not just save family items; she made sure that the past would not be forgotten by writing about it. She wrote a lengthy autobiography for her family. Her stories were also published. Her articles about growing up during the Great Depression on that dirt farm in the foothills of the Ozark Mountains were carried regularly in the *St. Joseph*

News Press during the 1970s. They are fun nostalgic pieces capturing family life during a bygone era.

In 2014, I flew to Missouri to speak at Aunt Avis's funeral. She was the last surviving member of Finn and Carrie's family. Although she was in her nineties, and I knew it was her time to go, when I stepped up to the pulpit to speak, I was overcome with emotion. I looked out at the other mourners. My sisters and cousins were in the audience. I thought, *The torch has been passed to our generation. We are now the keepers of the family stories, of the shared memories.*

My cousin Ruth was among the mourners that day. She was the oldest McCluey grandchild. She also wrote. Over the last several years, she sent me long letters full of her memories. Her prose contained very descriptive paragraphs about our grandparents' home and was full of emotion when she described the summer of 1960, with its back-to-back funerals. Aunt Avis's funeral was the last time I saw Ruth. I had just written the last line of this book when the phone rang. It was Carry, wishing me a happy birthday. She followed these words with some very sad ones: "I just got a phone call. Ruth passed away this morning." I hung up the phone and it immediately rang again. It was Lou Ann's voice that I heard. We also talked about Ruth. My older sister reminded me that July is a difficult month for our family. Our father, mother, grandfather, and now Ruth all passed away in the hot heat of a July Missouri day.

I sat alone for a while, thinking about our family. I regret that Ruth did not have the chance to read how I incorporated her memories into this narrative. I have finished writing our stories. Our memories are preserved. *Rest in peace, dear cousin.*

Sources

The *Little House* Books

I am not going to attempt to provide a complete bibliography for Laura Ingalls Wilder and her *Little House* books. Since there is a cottage industry based on Laura's writings, a complete listing would take several pages. I would be remiss if I did not list the children's classics in order of their publication:

> *Little House in the Big Woods*, 1932
> *Farmer Boy*, 1933
> *Little House on the Prairie*, 1935
> *On the Banks of Plum Creek*, 1937
> *By the Shores of Silver Lake*, 1939
> *The Long Winter*, 1940
> *Little Town on the Prairie*, 1941
> *These Happy Golden Years*, 1943
> *The First Four Years*, 1971,
> > published posthumously by Harper & Row

Collectively they are referred to as the *Little House* books. The first three books, published in the 1930s by Harper & Brothers, were illustrated by Helen Sewell. Mildred Boyle worked with Sewell to illustrate the first editions of the other five original books; however, the editions that I read during my childhood in that big white clapboard house were released in the 1950s and were illustrated by Garth Williams.

A few years ago for Christmas, my husband bought me a hardcover box set of all the books released in 2012 by the Library of America. It was a scholarly publication containing detailed footnotes, annotations, and explanations by Caroline Fraser. Fraser carefully compared Laura's handwritten drafts with the published version. This set was aimed at adults "who last enjoyed them as children {and} may be astonished at the quiet poetry of Wilder's prose and the force and poignancy of her portrait of the lives of American pioneers." There are no illustrations in this release. I admire Fraser's scholarship and attention to detail, but feel that she lost a little of the romance and fun of the books.

Many young girls imagine that they are the pig-tailed Laura of the first five books, riding on the back of the covered wagon as it moves through the tall grass of the prairie. I never wanted to be that Laura. Instead, I wanted to be the teenage Laura of the last three books. I am drawn to one of these books on a wintry afternoon; however, this year I read aloud chapters of the *Little House in the Big Woods* to first graders at Mt. Holly Springs Elementary School. I was captivated along with the first graders. I decided that the next time I have a chance, I am going to reread the first five books.

On the Way Home, the diary of Laura and Almanzo's move from De Smet, South Dakota, to Mansfield, Missouri, edited and supplemented by Rose Wilder Lane, was the most relevant to this book. It was published in 1976 by HarperCollins, nineteen years after Laura died.

In 2014, the South Dakota State Historical Society released Laura's first attempt at writing her life's story. She wrote for adults, and titled it *Pioneer Girl*. It was rejected by publishers in the 1930s, so Laura rewrote it for children. The adult version is much grittier than the subsequent *Little House* books. Pamela Smith Hill's detailed annotation of Laura's original attempt of capturing her life story was printed in a beautiful large hardbound volume. To the surprise of the historical society, the first limited printing quickly sold, as did subsequent printings.

Many scholarly books have been written about Laura Ingalls Wilder and her classic series. Clearly, some were originally doctoral dissertations. I have never been too concerned about the continuing debate regarding Rose Wilder Lane's role in creating the books and her complicated relationship to her mother. I also really do not care if Rose had a lesbian relationship with Helen Dore Boylston, the author of the Sue Barton series, which I also loved. If others want to worry about these issues, there are many other articles and books for them; however, I should mention two historians who have written extensively about Laura Ingalls Wilder, her life, and her writings. Their scholarship is commendable.

William Anderson is an American author, historian, and lecturer. He states that his interest in the American frontier began after reading *Little House on the Prairie*. He is a director of the Laura Ingalls Wilder Home and Museum in Mansfield, Missouri. He lives and works as a teacher in Michigan. In September 2002, he was invited to the White House for the third of Laura Bush's American Authors Symposia. The First Lady, a former teacher and librarian, assembled scholars, authors, and historians for a conference on the frontier experience. Anderson's works include:

Laura Ingalls Wilder: A Biography, 2007

Laura Ingalls Wilder Country, 1995

A Little House Sampler, by Laura Ingalls Wilder (Author), Rose Wilder Lane (Author), and William T. Anderson (Editor), 1988

John E. Miller taught American history for three decades at South Dakota State University and is a foremost scholar on Wilder's books and life. His books include:

Becoming Laura Ingalls Wilder: The Woman behind the Legend, published by the University of Missouri Press in 1998

Laura Ingalls Wilder's Little Town: Where History and Literature Meet, 1994

Laura Ingalls Wilder and Rose Wilder Lane: Authorship, Place, Time, and Culture, 2016

Anderson and Miller provide depth and historic perspective; however, for pure fun, I recommend *The Wilder Life: My Adventures in the Lost World of Little House on the Prairie* by Wendy McClure. Not only did I identify with McClure's love for the *Little House* series and her obsessive nature, but she also made me laugh out loud. It is a great read.

Supporting Documentation

I am bound for the Promised Land.

The words for *Don't Leave the Farm, Boys*, were written by Clara F. Berry in 1871. Laura Ingalls Wilder quotes the chorus and one of the stanzas in the "First Four Years." According to Caroline Fraser, the song appears in the *Conqueror*, printed in 1880. This songbook appears to be the one used by the singing school in De Smet, South Dakota, where Laura and Almanzo attended school when they were courting. I found the full text in the sheet music collection of the Library of Congress Music for the Nation: American Sheet Music, ca. 1870–1885.

William McKendree Carleton was a popular and prolific poet until his death in 1912. He wrote "Over the Hill to the Poor House" in addition to the poem "Mortgage." Carleton's poems were most often about rural life, and his work is often quoted by historians to capture the realities of life on farms during the panic years of the 1890s.

Will L. Thompson wrote the words to "Golden Years Are Passing By" from *These Happy Golden Years*. Laura Ingalls

Wilder not only uses his phrase as the title for her last book in the original series, but she closes her story with his lines.

Historian Roger Grant's *Self-Help in the 1890's Depression*, published by Iowa State University Press in 1983, gives a comprehensive overview of the results on average people of the severe economic conditions during the panic years.

I found one of the best descriptions of the panic years in central Iowa in a memoir published by the State Historical Society of Iowa in its Annals of Iowa, Volume 38, Number 6 (Fall 1966). Rae M. Booth's *Memoirs of An Iowa Farm Girl* captures the experience of "those panic years," and describes burning corn for fuel and using butter to grease the wagon wheels. She was Grandma's Carrie's contemporary.

Coxey's Army: A Study of the Industrial Army Movement of 1894 by Donald L. McMurray was published by the University of Washington Press in 1929. The quote about the "heartbreaking nineties" is from McMurray's first chapter.

Other material on this short-lived protest movement that sounds so relevant to today's world can be found in the following publications:

> *Coxey's Army: An American Odyssey* was written by Carlos A. Schwantes and published by the University of Idaho Press in 1994.

> *Coxey's Army: Popular Protest in the Gilded Age* by Benjamin F. Alexander was published in 2015 as part of the *Eyewitness to History* series by the Johns Hopkins University Press.

The song "Go Join Coxey's Army" was written by O. DuBois in 1894 and is also part of the sheet music collection of the Library of Congress.

Through its *Chronicling America* project, the Library of Congress has digitized copies of the *Iowa State Bystander*, a Des Moines newspaper published from 1894 to 1916. I followed the march of Coxey's Army across the state and saw advertisements for the "last good land in the Corn Belt at low prices" in the edition published on November 29, 1895.

The State Historical Society of Missouri provided me with the twenty-two page railroad publication of *Among the Ozarks: The Land of the Big Red Apples*, originally published by the Kansas City, Fort Scott and Memphis Railroad.

Wait until the darkness is over.

I referred to several acclaimed publications for background information for both the Great Depression and World War II:

> *Freedom from Fear: The American People in Depression and War 1929-1945* was written by David M. Kennedy. It was published by the Oxford University Press in 1999. The book was awarded the 2000 Pulitzer Prize for History.

> *The Great Depression: America, 1929–1941* is a 1984 history of the Great Depression by historian Robert S. McElvaine. It is considered one of the classic studies of the Great Depression. The book has stayed constantly in print since its publication. A second edition was published in 1993, coinciding with the eight-part PBS television series *The Great Depression*, for which this book was a major resource.

The Hungry Years: A Narrative History of the Great Depression in America was written by T.H. Watkins. The paperback version was published by Holt Paperbacks in 1999.

The ratings for television shows in 1959 are posted on the internet website:

http://www.yearborn.net/The_Year_You_Were_Born_Top_TV_Shows_1950s/1959.html

Statistics regarding life expectancy came from the digital history website:

http://www.digitalhistory.uh.edu/disp_textbook.cfm?smtid=2&psid=3175

The importance of the Rh factor in blood type is discussed on the following websites:

http://www.discoveriesinmedicine.com/Ra-Thy/Rh-Factor.html

http://www.mayoclinic.org/tests-procedures/rh-factor/basics/why-its-done/prc-20013476

The history of the Woman's Christian Temperance Union (WCTU) can be found on its website:

https://www.wctu.org/

The line "Somebody told me Wall Street fell" is from "Song of the South," written by Bob McDill. It was recorded at least twice, with limited success, before Alabama turned it into a mega hit. In November 1988, the popular country group released it as part of their album *Southern Star*. The song reached number one on both the U.S. and Canadian country charts.

Statistics regarding the temperatures in Kansas City and St. Louis during the thirties can be found in articles online:

https://en.wikipedia.org/wiki/1936_North_American_heat_wave

http://www.stltoday.com/news/local/metro/a-look-back-relentless-withering-heat-wave-of-killed-in/article_3821b7be-14c4-5fef-b0c9-bc383d50aafd.html

http://www.kchistory.org/week-kansas-city-history/heat-wave

http://www.stltoday.com/news/local/metro/a-look-back-relentless-withering-heat-wave-of-killed-in/article_3821b7be-14c4-5fef-b0c9-bc383d50aafd.html

I hear the rolling thunder.

I was able to recreate life in Lockwood, Missouri, during World War II by reading articles printed in the *Lockwood Luminary* and compiled by Sue Sparkman. She published them in PDF format under the title *Lockwood, MO, Small Town USA, 1883-1979.*

"I'll Be Back In A Year (Little Darlin')" was recorded on January 22, 1941, by the Prairie Ramblers. It was written by Claude Heritier, Russ Hull, and Ben Shelhamer Jr. "I'll Be Waiting for You, Darling" was written by the same team as an answer song. It was released later in 1941 by the Prairie Ramblers, with Gale Ryan as the vocalist.

"My Dreams Are Getting Better All the Time" was released in 1945, toward the end of the war. It reached the Billboard charts on March 15, 1945, peaked at number one, and was still a Billboard hit on May 8, when the war ended in Europe. The music was written by Vic Mizzy and the lyrics by Manny Curtis. The hit song that played on Armed Services Radio was recorded by the Les Brown Orchestra, with a vocal by Doris Day.

My treasures are laid up somewhere beyond the blue.

Grand Expectations: The United States, 1945-1974, by James T. Patterson, was published by the Oxford University Press in 1986. It was awarded the 1997 Bancroft Prize. It captures the post-war years, the decade in which my father practiced medicine, and those years when I was a teenager.

The Glory and the Dream: A Narrative History of America, 1932-1972, by William Manchester, was first published in 1974. It provides interesting tidbits from the post-war era, including the story of the miniature plow on Truman's desk and the popularity of ice cream in 1946.

The Historical Society of Missouri provided papers from the University of Missouri, president's office. Relevant material for my parents' early married experience included enrollment statistics and issues related to housing concerns.

The Common Sense Book of Baby and Child Care by Benjamin Spock was first published in 1946. The book, along with Dr. Spock, attained fame almost instantly, selling 500,000 copies in its first six months. By Spock's death in 1998, over 50 million copies of the book had been sold, making it the bestselling book of the twentieth century in America, aside from the Bible. It was published by Duell, Sloan, and Pearce.

America in the Fifties, by Andrew J. Dunar, was published by the Syracuse University Press in 2006.

Great Expectations: America's Baby Boom Generation was written by Landon Jones. The paperback edition was published in 2008 by by BookSurge Publishing.

"What a Friend We Have in Jesus" was written by Joseph M. Scriven as a poem in 1855 to comfort his mother when they were apart. Scriven originally published the poem anonymously and only received full credit for it in the 1880s. The tune to the hymn was composed by Charles Crozat Converse in 1868.

I come to the garden alone.

Gertrude Chandler Warner's *The Boxcar Children* was first published by Rand McNally and Company in 1924, but it was rewritten completely in 1942 with a vocabulary aimed at children. In 1949, Warner brought out the second book in the series, *Surprise Island*. She contributed nineteen more books to the series before she passed it on to other authors. Now there are approximately 130 titles in the *Boxcar Children* series.

"A birdie with a yellow bill" is from the poem "Time to Rise," and the "In Winter I get up at night" is the first line of "Bed in summer." Both poems are by Robert Louis Stevenson and are printed in his *A Child's Garden of Verses*. This collection of classic children's rhymes was first printed in 1885, but has been reprinted many times.

The Honorable William S. Richards, Associate Circuit Judge for the 4th Circuit Court in Holt County, Missouri, confirmed my memories of election night in Holt County during the 1970s. His father was also an elected official during that time, and Ed Richard's vote counts were also posted on the blackboard.

The statistics from the election night came from the *Holt County Sentinel*. My mother saved the printed tallies, and I found them in one of her boxes.

The Hymns behind the Section Titles

Blest Be the Tie: "Blest Be the Tie That Binds" was written by John Fawcett, a British-born Baptist theologian, pastor, and hymn writer. This is his most famous hymn and was published in 1782. It is included in most Protestant hymnals.

This Is My Story, This Is My Song: The line begins the refrain of the classic hymn "Blessed Assurance" and was written in 1873 by blind hymn writer Fanny Crosby to music created by Phoebe Knapp. It has become a beloved hymn among many Protestants and has been recorded by artists over the years, including Glenn Campbell, Alan Jackson, and Cece Winans.

I Am Bound for the Promised Land. The refrain from "On Jordan's Stormy Banks I Stand" was written by Samuel Stennett in 1787. It is a standard in gospel collections, and has been recorded by Jars of Clay and Bill and Gloria Gaither.

Wait Until the Darkness Is Over: This line appears in the first stanza of "Whispering Hope," written by Septimus Winner in 1868. The writer released much of his work under the pseudonym Alice Hawthorne. It has been recorded by many artists, including Anne Murray and Pat Boone.

I Hear the Rolling Thunder: The line is from the classic hymn "How Great Thou Art." It extols the splendor and greatness of God's creation, and was first written in Swedish by Carl Gustav Boberg in 1885. His words were translated into German, then into Russian, and subsequently into English by missionary Stuart K. Kline. Kline added two original verses of his own. The hymn was sung by George Beverly Shea and Cliff Barrows during the Billy Graham crusades.

My Treasures Are Laid Up Somewhere Beyond the Blue: The second line of the gospel song "This World Is Not My Home" was written by Albert E. Brumley and published originally in 1937. Most recently it was recorded by Jim Reeves.

I Come to the Garden Alone: The first line of the hymn "In the Garden" was written by American songwriter C. Austin Miles and first published in 1912. It was popularized during the revivals of evangelist Billy Sunday that were held during the second decade of the twentieth century. Later it was recorded by many artists, including Elvis Presley, Willie Nelson, Rosemary Clooney, and Perry Como.

A Conversation
with the Author

It's interesting that your Missouri Trilogy was written out of order. Will you describe how this evolved?

Blest be the Tie is the third book of my Missouri trilogy. Although it is the last of the three that I wrote, it is both a prequel and a sequel to the other two books in the series. The books are tied together by the same major characters, my parents and their children. They are also linked together by Missouri, the land where they lived. There is a major issue that is the backdrop for each book in the trilogy: health care, education policy, and the role of women. Each of these issues was part of the national debate the year that I wrote the book. Flowing throughout the trilogy is the idea that world and political events affect average people and change their lives.

Unpacking Memories, the first book in the trilogy, was released in 2013 as the debate over Obamacare and its passage brought health care to the forefront of our national discussions. Set in the 1950s in a small town in rural Missouri, the book is an evocative description of life during that decade and centers around stories of my father, a county doctor. Doc Sweaney made house calls, was paid with bushels of tomatoes, and died much too young. It is also the story of a tightknit community, Oregon, the county seat of rural Holt County, Missouri.

In Up in the Air, I return to the same county. It is now the mid-1960s. America is changing, and even in rural Missouri life is disrupted. The county is rocked by a school consolidation fight that threatens to change the way of life for people living in two neighboring communities. I was drawn to this issue after being elected to the Carlisle Area School District Board. American public schools were once controlled by elected local school boards who represented the community values. Now schools are professionally run bureaucracies controlled to a large extent by policies created at the state or national level. These changes can be traced to the middle 1960s.

The final book in the trilogy, *Blest Be the Tie,* focuses on the story of four generations of women in my mother's family. This book covers a larger time period and is more ambitious and sweeping than the other two books. Each woman is nothing special. There are women like them in most American families. I use their stories to tell the story of America and the changing role of American women from the 1870's through the 1970's. Anna, my great-grandmother, was part of the western migration into America's heartland. My grandmother came of age during the Temperance movement, before women had the right to vote. My mother is of the "greatest generation" living through both the Great Depression and World War II, and I am a baby boomer.

It is the story of my parents, my grandparents, and their parents. I tell of the land where they lived, rural Missouri, in the last decades of the nineteenth and into the late twentieth centuries. They are not perfect people. They made mistakes and bad decisions. But through all the hard times, they persevered. I write because I do not want them to be forgotten. They lived America's story and the events that we now call history. This is not just family lore, but is based on extensive research in both primary and secondary resources.

Did you encounter any obstacles along the way in writing this book?

I am not a natural writer. I find it hard work. I come from a long line of story-tellers and I had to learn to translate that verbal gift into writing. With this third book, I think I am getting better at it. At least, I hope so.

There was an emotional price in writing each of these books. I opened up old wounds. In the process, I emerged as a new person. In some cases, I relived painful events. It made my writing more powerful, but it took a toll on me at times. My goal was never to hurt anyone. These are real people in my books, some still alive. If they are gone, their descendants are still alive. On a few occasions, I found myself rewriting a section or paragraph to keep it from sounding harsh or judgmental.

In the end, I found all three books to be a healing, cathartic, experience. In healing my own wounds, I had to be aware that my family members and, in some cases, people outside my own family also carried their own wounds. I tried to be sensitive to each person's process in dealing with the events and their interpretation of the story. However, I had to write these books. It was almost as if I had no choice.

The women in your book all endured challenges, not the least of which was your mother, Iris who had to raise four children alone. Can you describe the kind of strength it took for her to walk through her grief and carry on as the strong an inspiring mother that she was?

For much of my childhood, my mother was grieving my father's death. She went through all the stages of grief including what I now see as depression. She came through her own garden "alone" and emerged a stronger woman.

When I was a girl, I thought I needed to help take care of her. Now, I see her as one of the strongest women I have ever known. She walked her road with the support of her sister Avis and some caring friends. However, she found strength deep inside herself. In her note that she wrote on her sixty-fifth birthday, she gave my father credit for her ability to carry on alone. It was typical of my mother. She was incredibly modest and never acknowledged her own gifts. Nurtured by her faith and driven to give her children a better life, Iris McCluey Sweaney not only persevered but eventually triumphed.

How would you like readers to understand the lives of the women in your family in terms of the struggles and hardships that they faced?

At times it was a challenge not to put my twenty-first century sensibilities into the stories of Anna, Carrie, and Iris. We need to be careful about judging people by the values of our times. These women were real people who were influenced by their beliefs. We may not agree with these values or beliefs; however, we must accept that their world view was influenced by their circumstances and traditions.

I may want to put my Grandma Carrie in another place, to give her a chance to develop her talent. But do I have any right to assume that she was unhappy with her life as a mother? Worldly success, achievement, and empowerment – as we define them in the twenty-first century – cannot be equated with happiness and fulfillment.

What do you hope your audience will take away from your story?

First and foremost, I hope people enjoy the story. The people in my books are real, not creations of my imagination. They may not be special or powerful, but I try to paint them as three-dimensional individuals. They once lived, loved, and grieved. Many people will see women of their own family in the story of Anna, Carrie, or Iris. In reading my family story, I hope people will remember their own stories and the women who came before them. We stand on their shoulders.

About the Author

Photo by Marc Foubel

Deborah Sweaney lives in Carlisle, Pennsylvania. It seems at times far away from her roots in Missouri, but she is reminded that both her McCluey and Swartz ancestors once called Pennsylvania home. She moved to Washington, D.C., just after college to intern for Missouri Representative Jerry Litton, and Washington remained her home for the next thirty years. She worked for multiple government agencies, including an internship with the planning organization for the Richard Nixon Presidential Library and Museum, the White House Office of Records Management, and finally with the Federal Deposit Insurance Corporation (FDIC). She and her husband left Washington, D.C., for Carlisle, Pennsylvania, in 2006. In her words, "After 9/11, the security in the city was so overwhelming it no longer seemed like fun to be there."

For Sweaney, history extends beyond the personal. In 2010, she established her own company, Ancestry Searches, and helps others find their own family treasures. She is a member of several professional associations dedicated to the study of history. In addition, she is a former adjunct instructor at Messiah College, the University of the District of Columbia, and Marymont University in Arlington, Virginia, and has been a consultant for National History Day. She is a frequent lecturer on the joys of family history research.

She is committed to public education and ensuring that young people have the academic opportunities to thrive. She looks no further than her own parents' stories to understand the difference that education can make for a family. With proceeds from *Unpacking Memories*, Sweaney's book that honors the 1950s in Holt County, Missouri, and her parents' memory, she established the Iris and Frank Sweaney Fund. The fund awards scholarships, offers educational programs, and provides other financial incentives for Holt County young people. Proceeds from her second book, *Up in the Air*, also supported this fund, as will sales from this book.

Now, in her new community, she continues to support public education of young people as an elected official on the Carlisle Area School District Board.

WA